# Letters of EMPOWERMENT

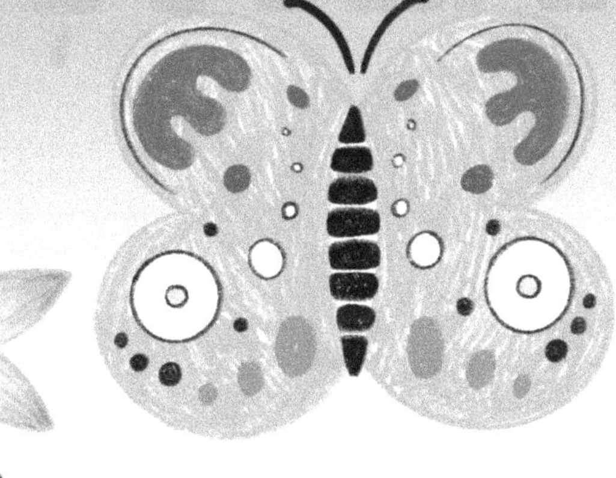

Mariia Biriukova

♦ SELF-CONFIDENCE AND SELF-ESTEEM ♦

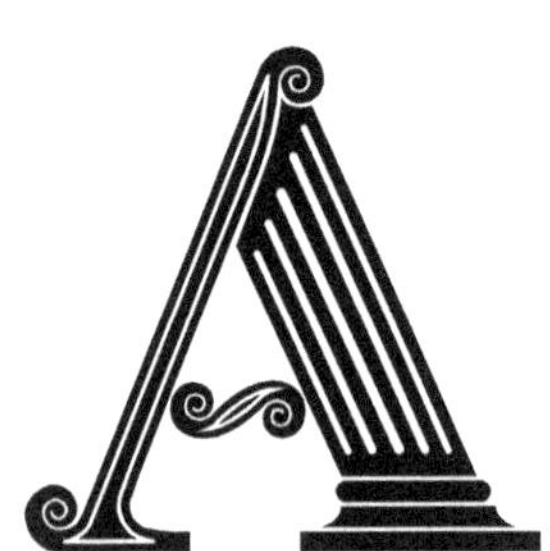

Letters of Empowerment

*A Journey of Self-Discovery Through Lettering, Coloring, and Personal Growth Projects*
© 2024 by Special Art



For permissions, contact: support@specialartbooks.com

Published by Special Art Books | www.specialartbooks.com

Paperback ISBN: 9791255531999

Images © Shutterstock

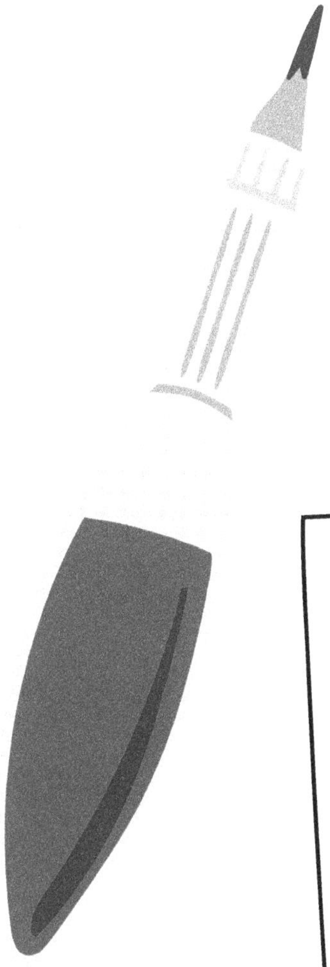

This book
belongs to

. . . . . . . . . . . . . . . . . . . . . . . . . . . . . . . . . . . . . . . . . .

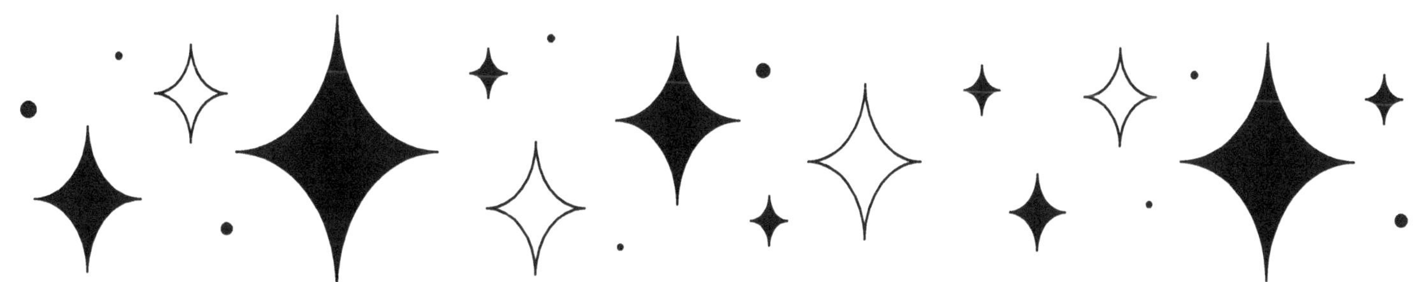

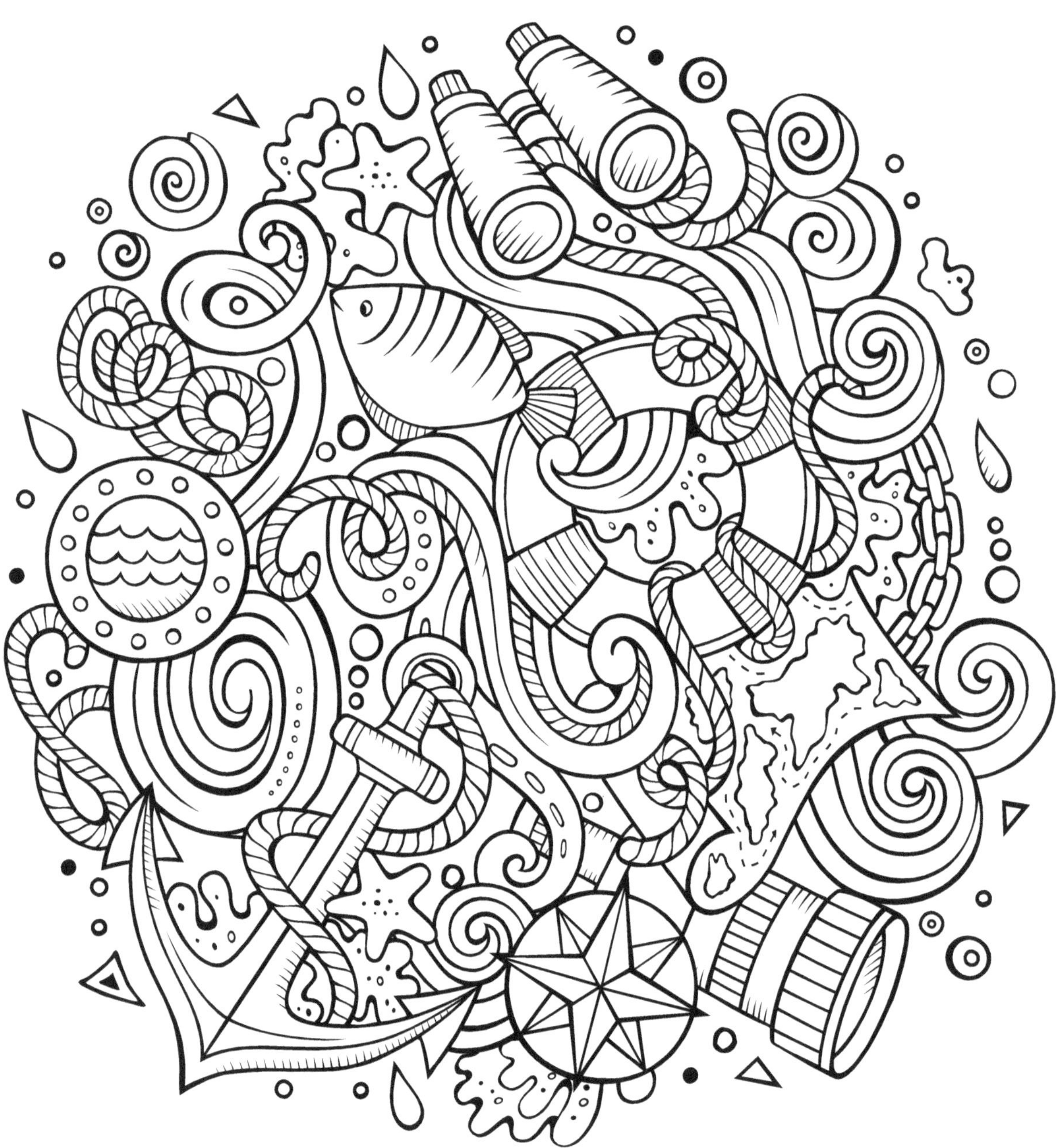

# TABLE OF CONTENTS



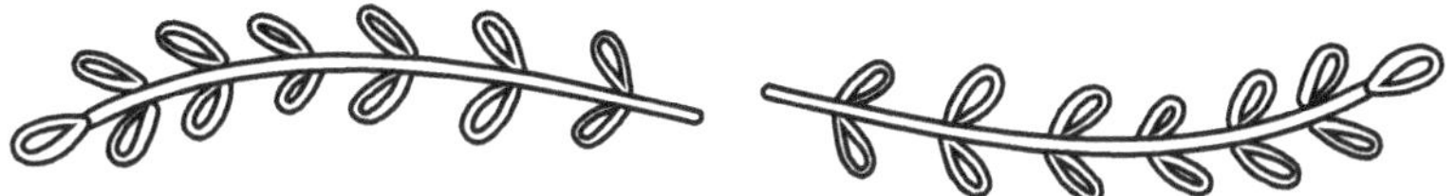

# INTRODUCTION

You are an amazing person, capable of so many things, including expressing your emotions through lettering and creativity. You are already empowered to bring your dreams and ambitions into reality, taking steps through art and calligraphy. Recognize your worth and your value. Welcome to *Letters of Empowerment*.

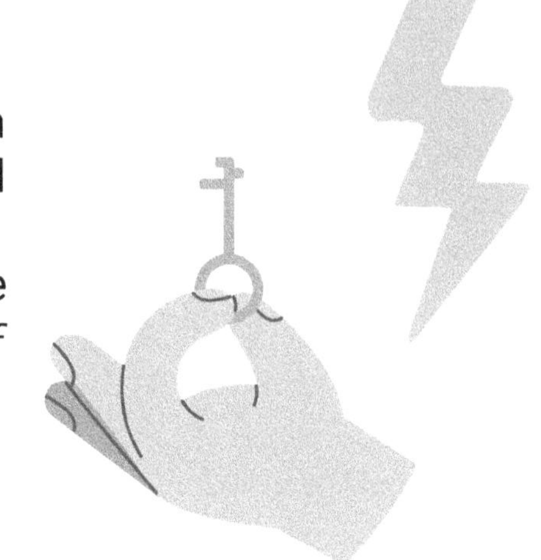

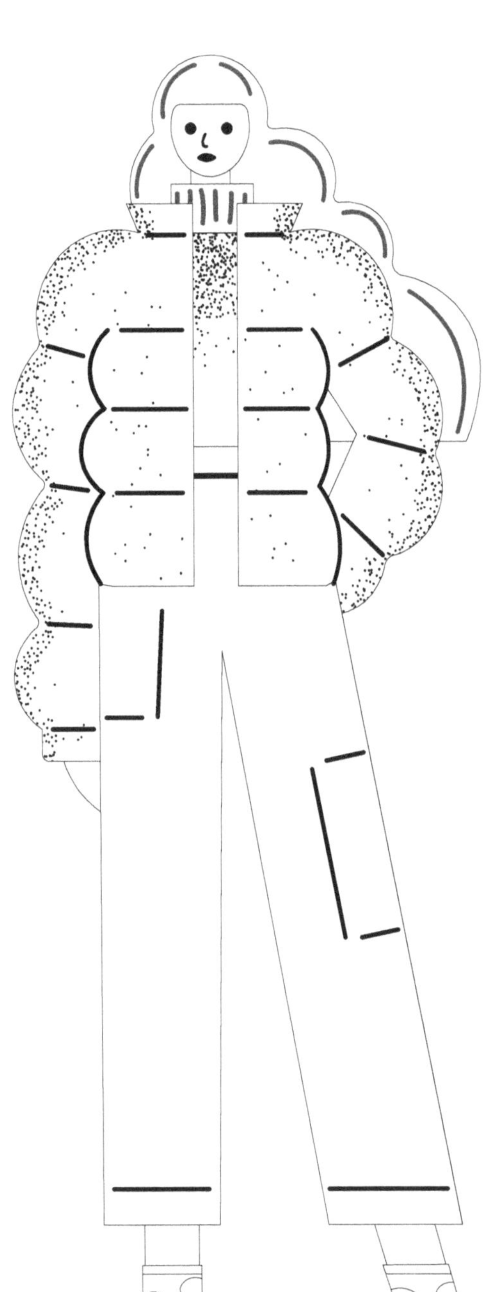

In this book, you'll learn how to empower yourself, changing your mindset into one of openness, developing your own decisiveness, and creating an environment wherein you are free to be as authentic as you want. The creative exercises and projects in this book use a range of lettering styles, colors, and inspirational quotes to guide you into reflecting and expressing what you truly feel about your own strength and power.

Throughout *Letters of Empowerment*, you will learn not only to write beautifully but to also write truthfully about who you are, about who you want to be, and about how you want to get to where you want to be. The art you will create as a result of this book will also help you support the people in your life who also need to find their power to grow and thrive.

As you start this journey, you'll learn skills and new techniques to showcase your creativity. We'll start from the basics and move into practical applications for you to see your own progress in the real world.

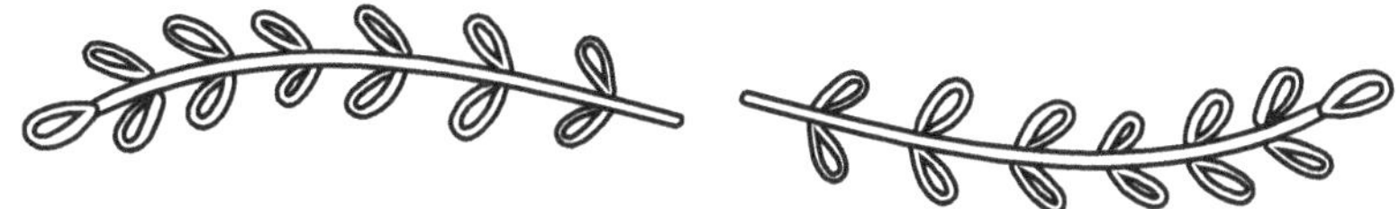

*What does empowerment look like?*
We see this word attached to many subjects but how do we translate this into something we can visualize? When drawing objects, for example, we already have an idea on how it looks. But drawing or lettering the elements of empowerment would be different. In this book, we will gradually define what it consists of, and we will learn how to notice it and how to cultivate it.

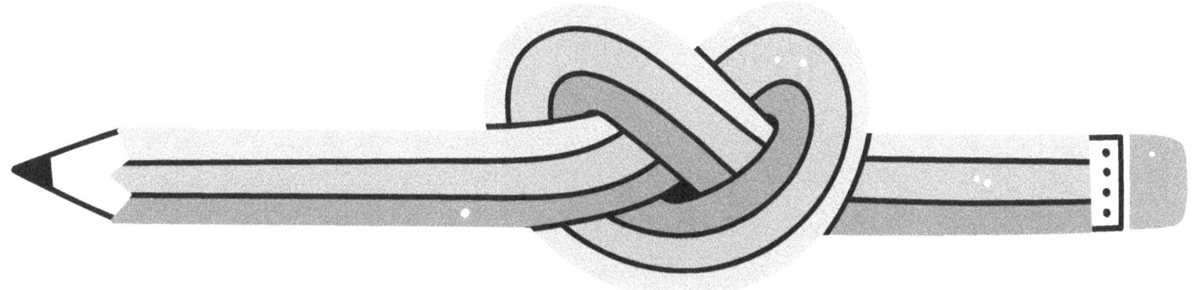

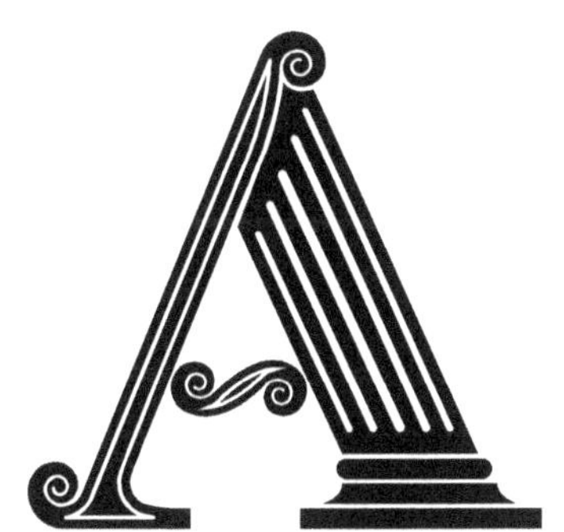

How does empowerment relate to art?
Whenever you look at paintings or sculptures or monuments, what do you see? What emotions does the art make you feel? Visualizing power into works of art affects people through generations. It does not only help the viewers, but it lets the artist heal and express their soul. This is how you can also empower yourself.

*In this book, we will express empowerment, using calligraphy and coloring. Getting started with calligraphy is actually not as hard as it seems.*

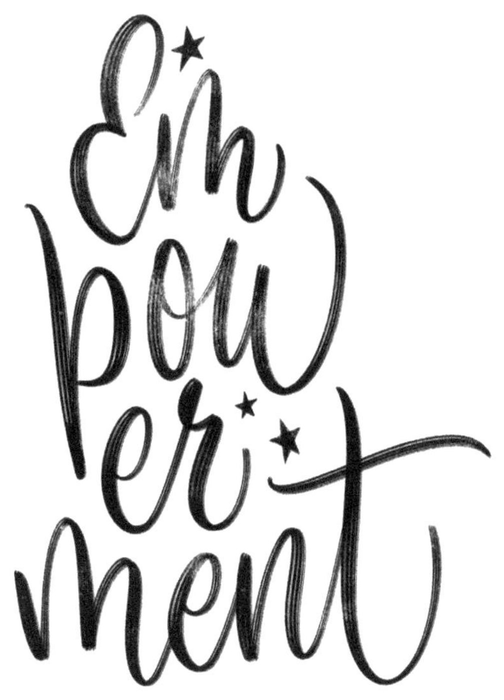


There is a difference between calligraphy and lettering. While calligraphy is commonly known as the art of beautiful writing, lettering is actually drawing the letters in different shapes and styles. Both will depend on the tools, movements of the hand, and the artist's main idea that can be conveyed through the art.

When creating unique written art, remember that your emotions and thoughts are transferred to the page or media that you choose. The shapes of the letters or the smoothness of the strokes can tell your audience a message that is beyond text. There are techniques that will help you connect to your audience.

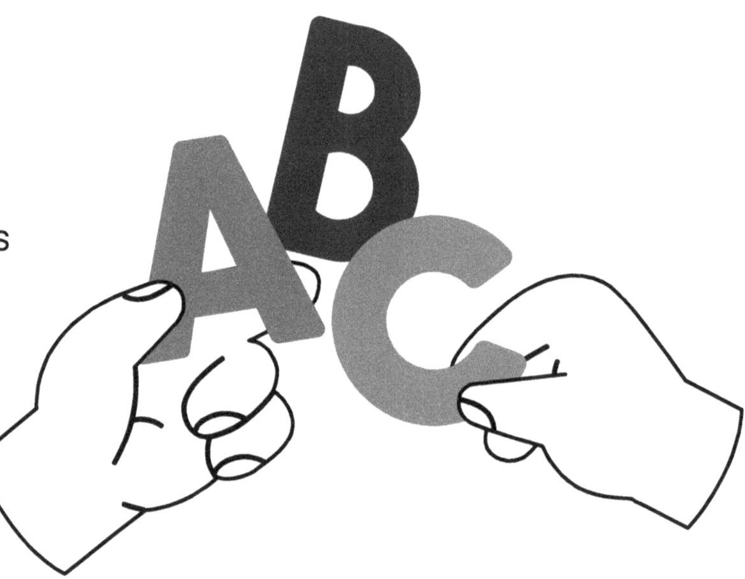


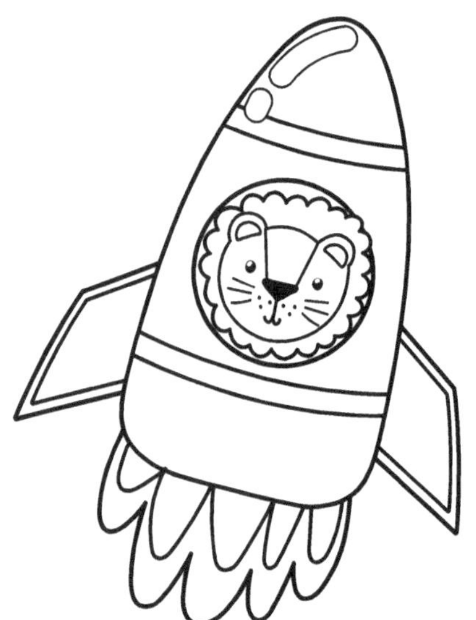

But both calligraphy and lettering have the task of creating unique pieces of art that create the atmosphere and mood of a phrase before you read the letters.

Actually - any typeface has a shape and creates a certain look - but the fonts that are used for large blocks of text are designed to make the reading experience as comfortable as possible. If you're reading a book and you're not paying attention to the typeface, it's a good type. But the opposite is true of display fonts - a neutral sign on the street will not catch the eye or attract customers.

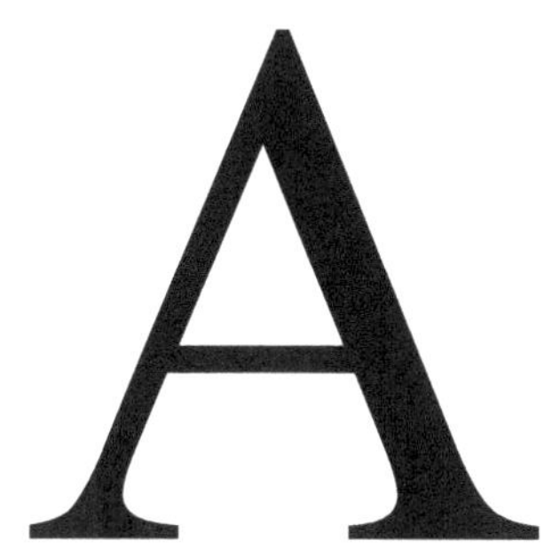

*The shape of the letters should always match the task and the meaning.*

As we cultivate our empowerment, we must strive for strong, bold images. We should use all options for this - bold strokes, free forms. Don't be afraid to break the rules, you make the rules here, and it can be as you want it to be!

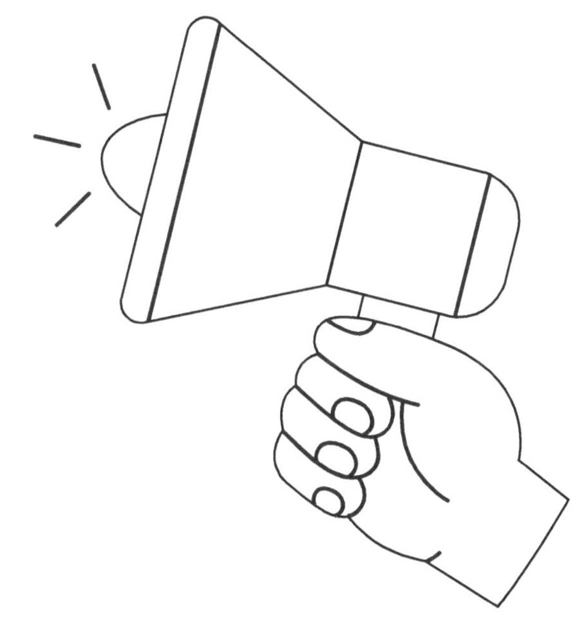

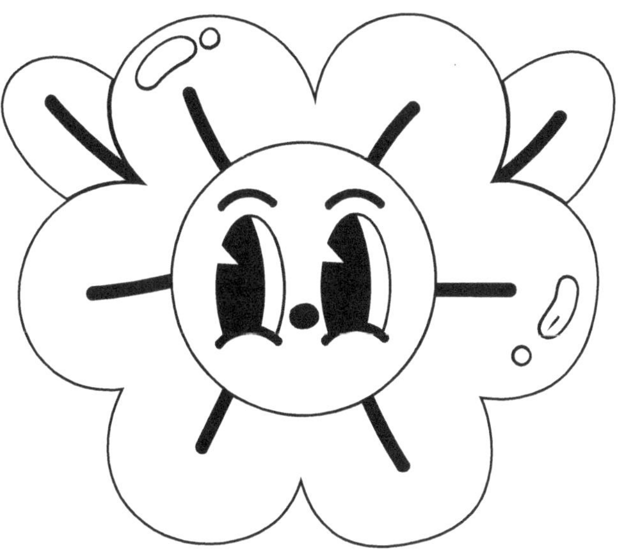

Personal empowerment is about taking control of your own life and making positive decisions based on what you want and what you like. Focus on the process, not the result.

Now let's talk about what you need and the writing instruments that can get you started in this empowering journey.

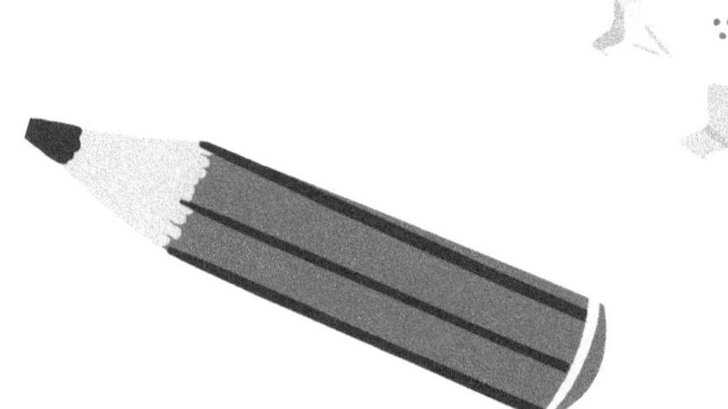

The pages of this book are created for you to color with pencils, markers, or watercolors. You can find these in your local stores or you can use whatever you already have available.

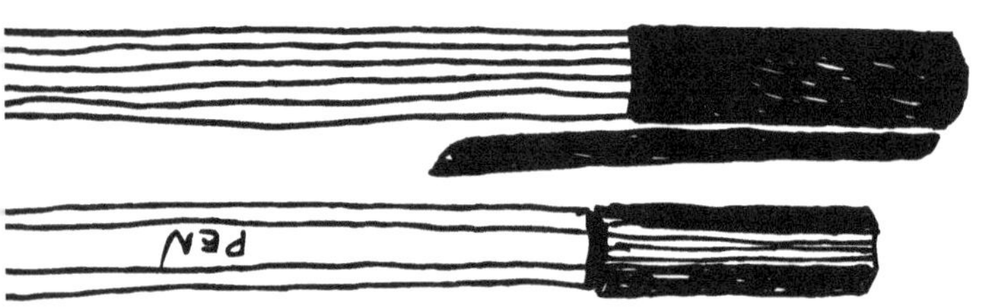



Since we won't be using classic calligraphy, there's no need to use the nib and ink (but you can always try the exercises on a more absorbent paper). This book will focus on your hand movements and, in the later pages, will let you write freely in your own style.

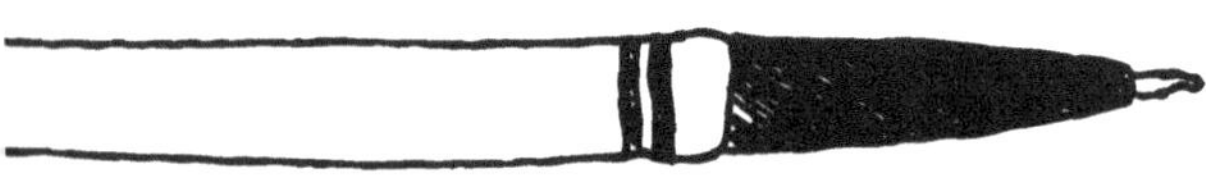

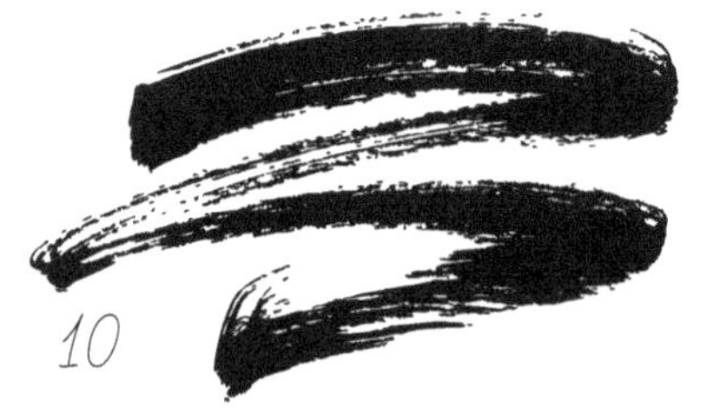

*Creativity is always an open field for experimentation. You are the artist.*

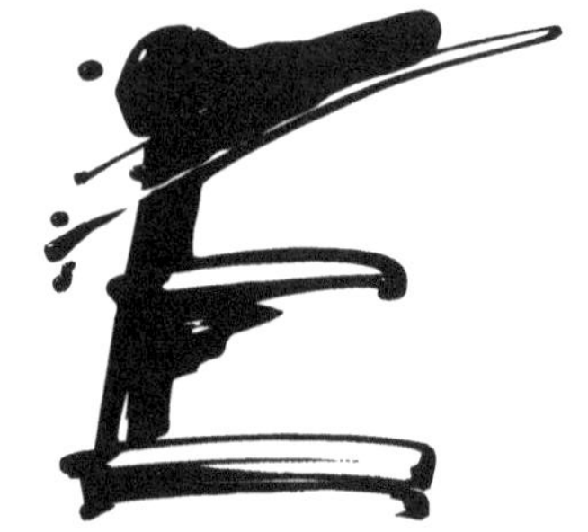

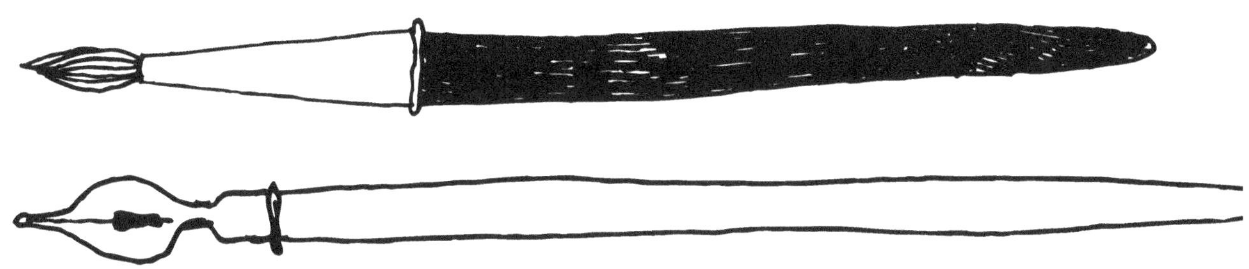

Every artist started as a beginner. As beginners, mistakes, smudges, and color bleeds can happen. That's okay. It's part of the process and part of how you can reach your own style. For color bleeds, we recommend placing a save sheet or scrap paper between the pages while coloring to protect your other pages of art.

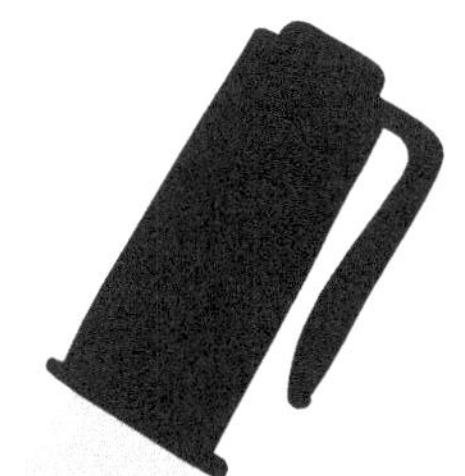

Mistakes and unplanned strokes can also become part of your art. Embrace these learning moments and use what you know for your future work. These are opportunities for growth and self-empowerment.

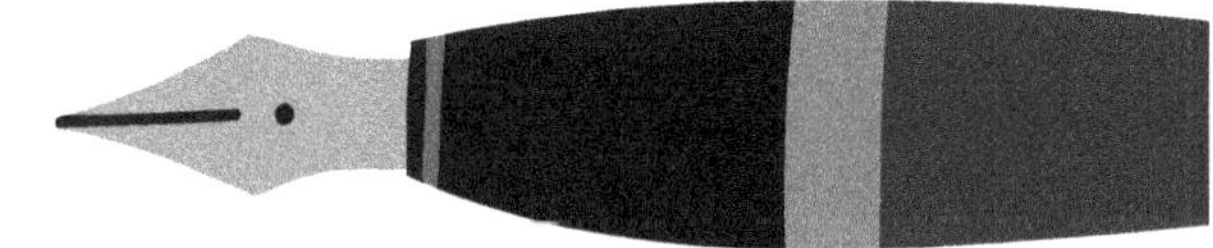

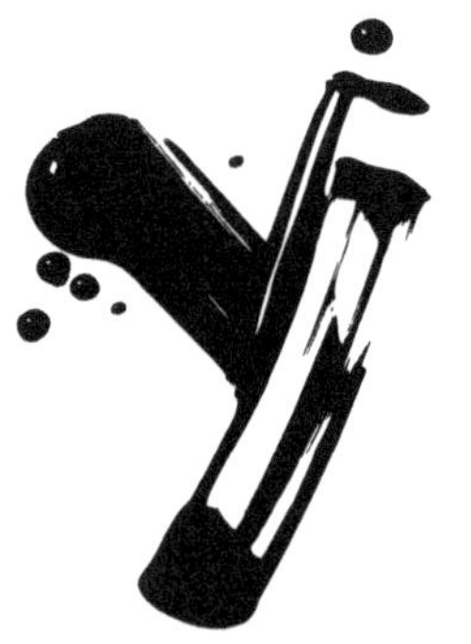

To enhance your coloring experience, consider using a removable and foldable coloring workspace made from thicker paper or cardboard. This workspace can be attached to the book spine or included in an envelope on the back cover. Featuring inspirational quotes and motifs related to the book's theme, the visually appealing workspace can serve as an added layer of protection and inspiration while coloring.

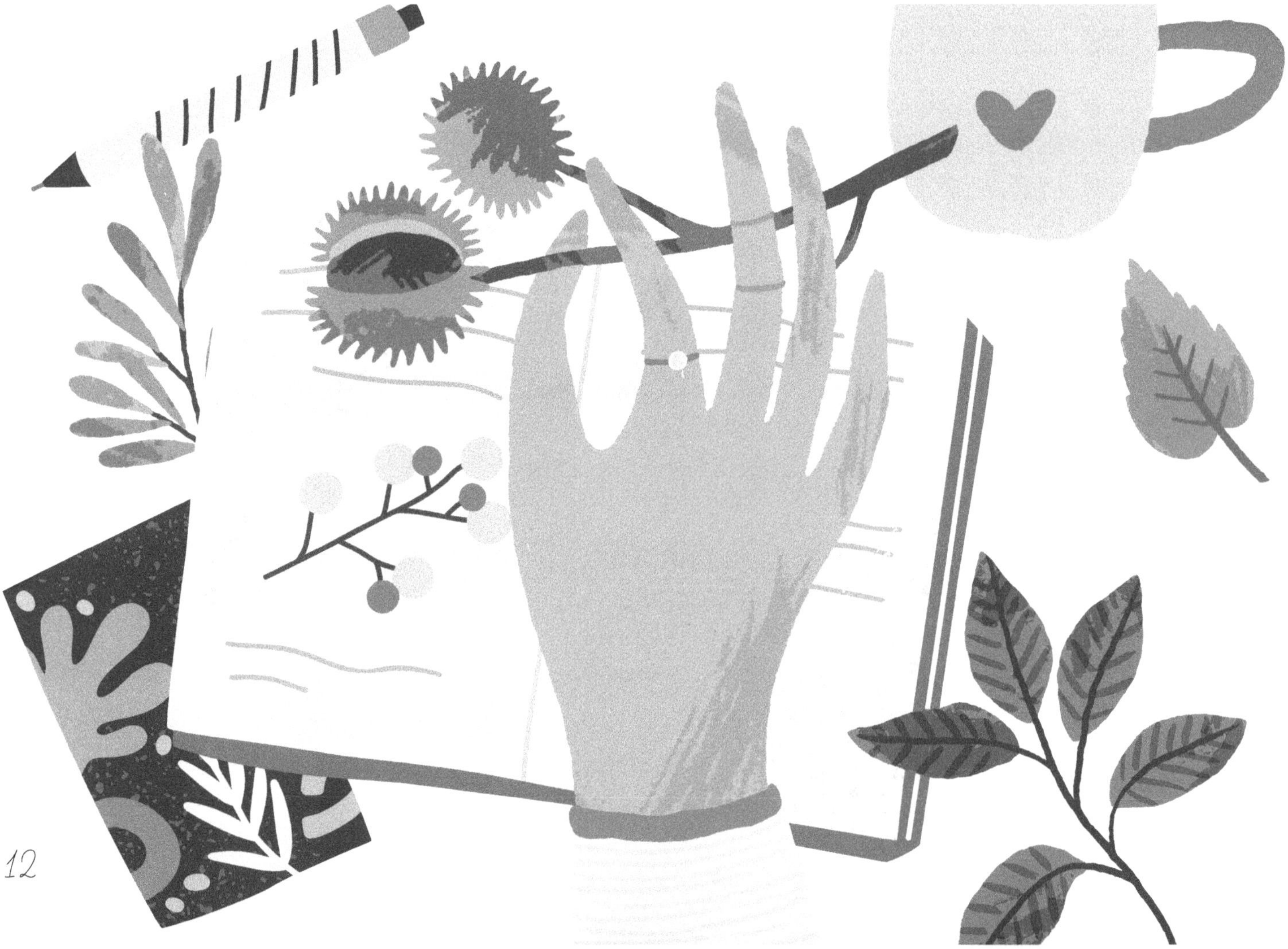

*Discipline and goal achievement are very good in developing strength and empowerment. This book will help you a lot with that! Here are some tips on how to make the most of your time with this book:*

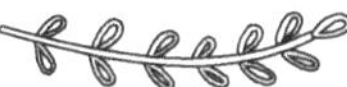

✦ Choose a time to work on these exercises and stick to a schedule.

✦ Make sure no one can distract you.

✦ Find a comfortable space where you can work. Organize everything conveniently so that you can use your available materials and practice new techniques easily.

✦ Set a goal and make your time with this book intentional. When you complete a section, take time to rest and reflect on your achievement.

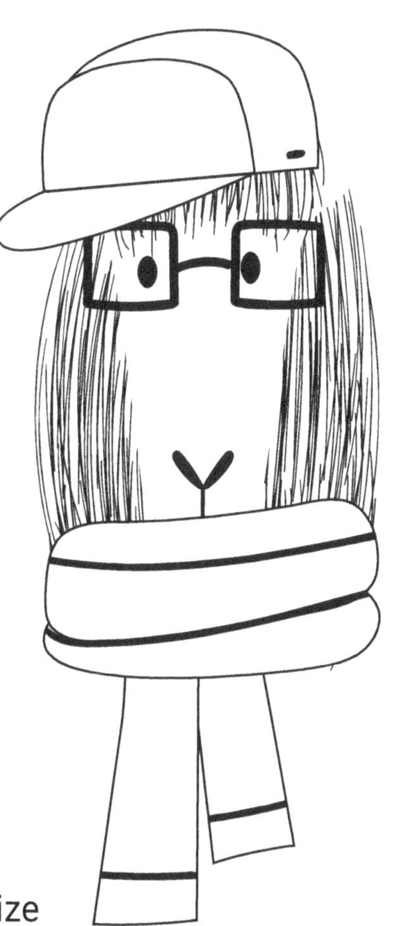

Now it's time for you to start on this journey. This is a safe space, so let the empowered version of yourself shine through. See how art and creativity can transform your life. Welcome to *Letters of Empowerment*!

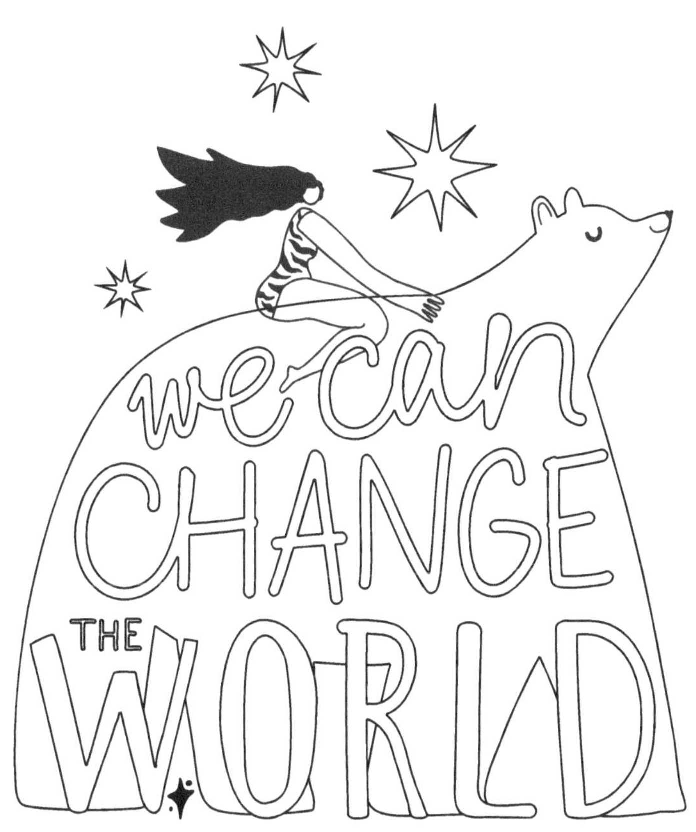

# COLORS AND LINES

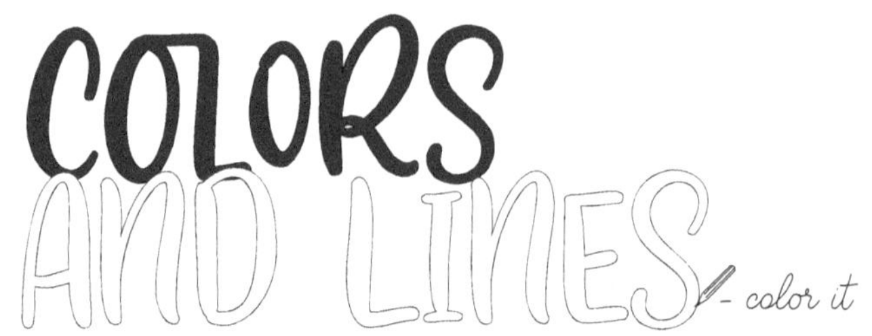


Color is an important element in any kind of art. The colors of a masterpiece usually reflect either the feelings of the artist while they are creating it or the emotions that the artist wants to convey to the observers. As you start to discover intentional and empowered living, we will start with some color exercises to hone your emotions and expressions.

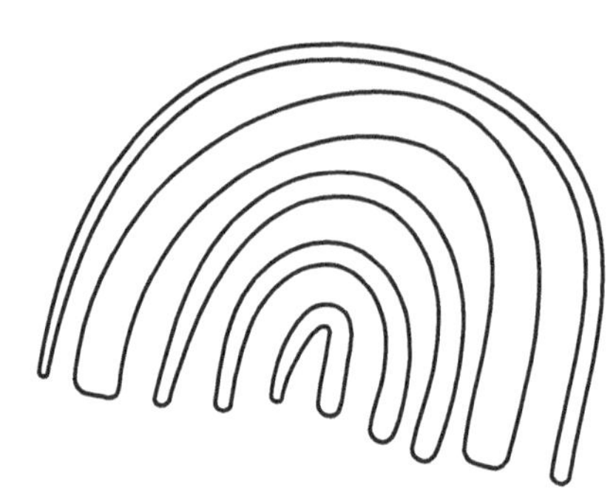

When was the last time you felt empowered to do something? What did you do that made you realize you can do things you never thought you could before? What colors do you associate with that memory? Think of the color palette in that memory and use it to set yourself up for that feeling of empowerment.

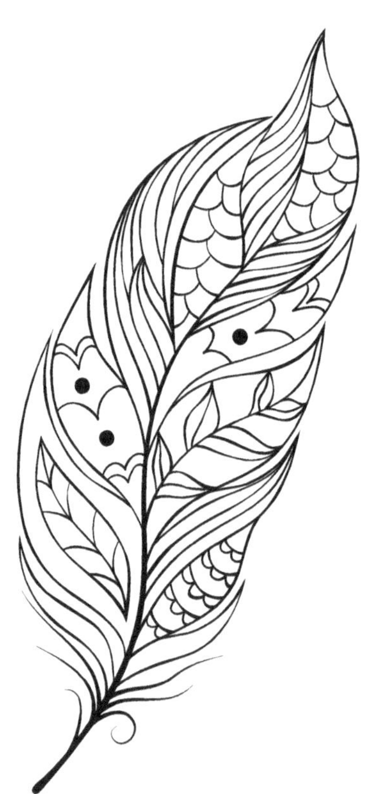

- *Blue* is the color of tranquility, freedom, and infinity

- *Orange* color produces a joyful impression, the desire to move, activates action

- *Magenta* has the royal qualities of power and majesty.

Color meanings don't exist in a vacuum; there are lots of factors that impact how we perceive them. Some of these factors include:

- Their shade, tint, or tone

- How they're combined with other colors

- Their saturation

- How they're paired with other design elements like fonts and shapes.

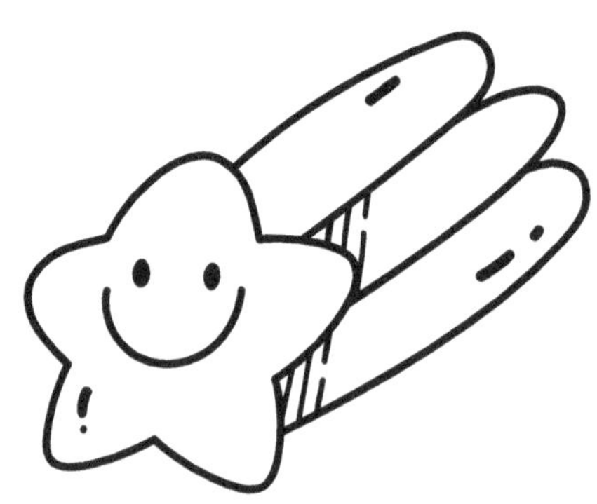



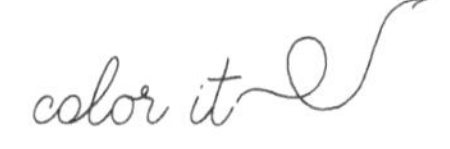

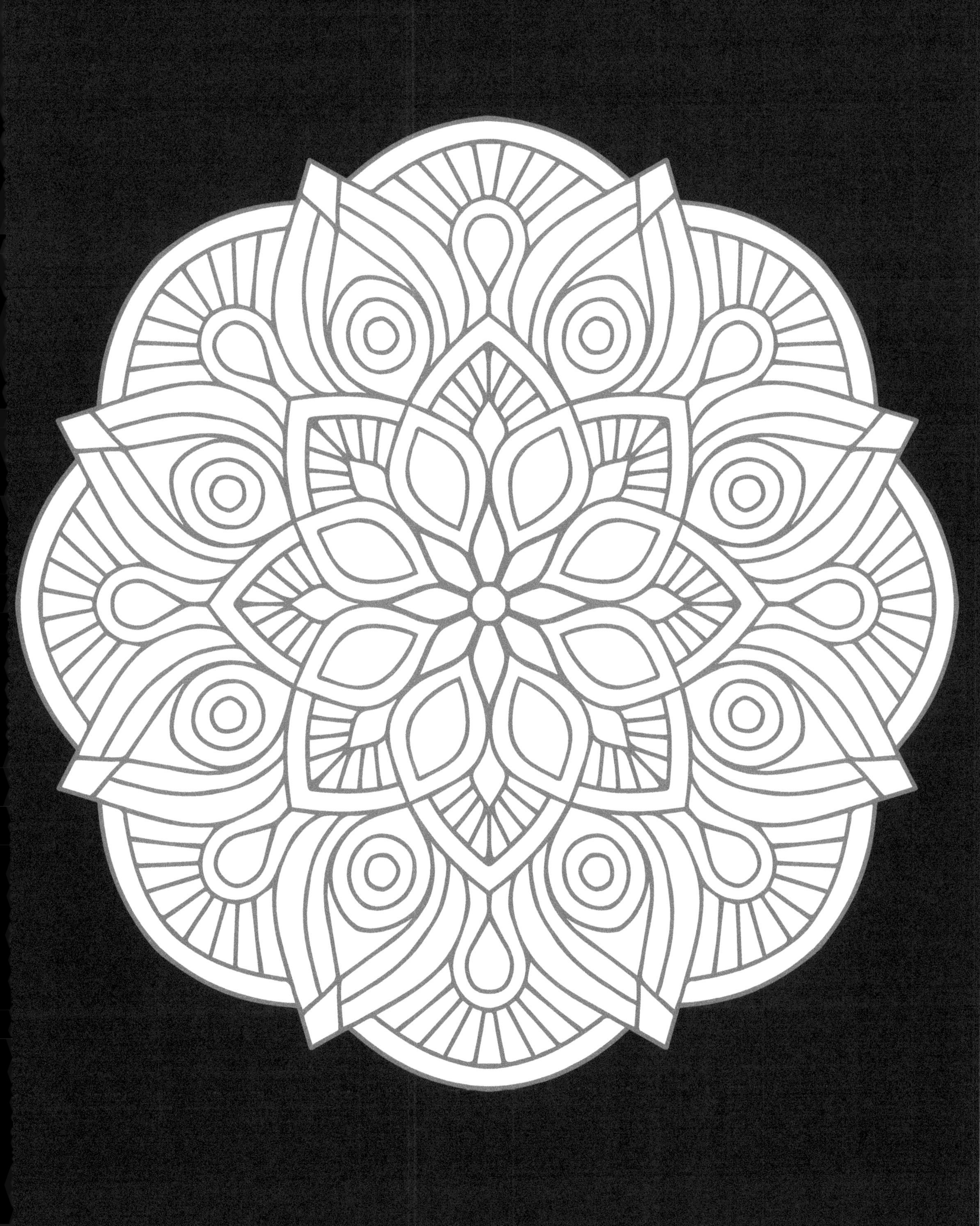

One of the most important expressive tools is the line. A line can convey form, many lines can create tone. Let's take a closer look at the expressive possibilities of the line.

A line expresses character. It can be rough and sharp, soft and smooth, light and playful.

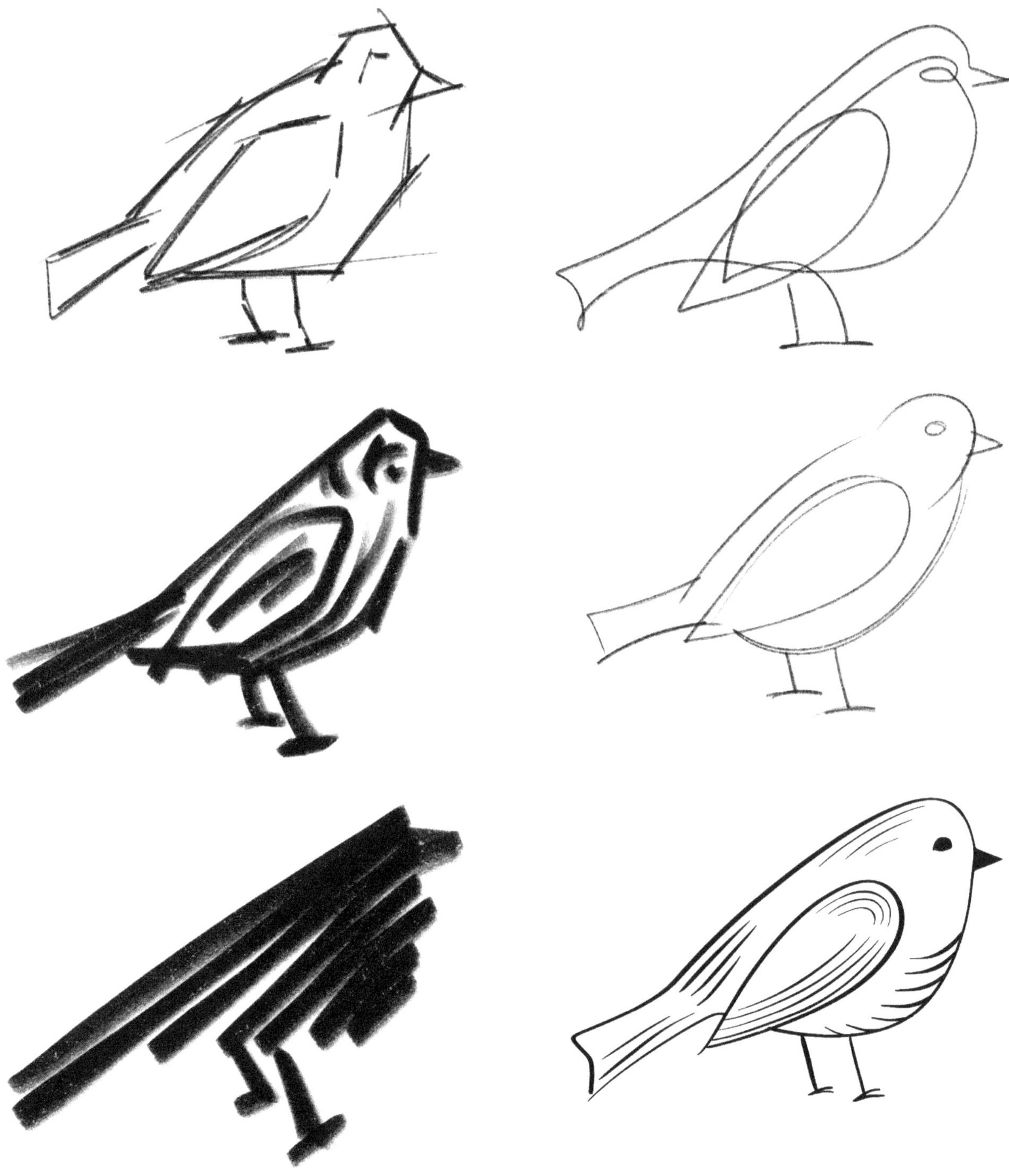

If you're coloring with a pencil, you're also using lines to get the right density of color. If you arrange the lines chaotically, it will be difficult to control the contrast in the image.

Try to place the lines in one direction, first at a short distance and with light pressure, then fill in the gaps and increase the pressure.
To get a denser color add lines at a slightly different angle, but not perpendicular.

Let's try to make a smooth transition from white to black in 6 steps.

Repeat these exercises before drawing and you will see how much
easier it will be for you to control everything that happens on the paper.

To learn to draw lines with different personalities,
try to hold the pencil differently and move your
hand lightly.

✦ For long, smooth lines hold your hand freely
and move from the shoulder.

✦ For rounded lines use the movement
from the elbow.

Experiment!

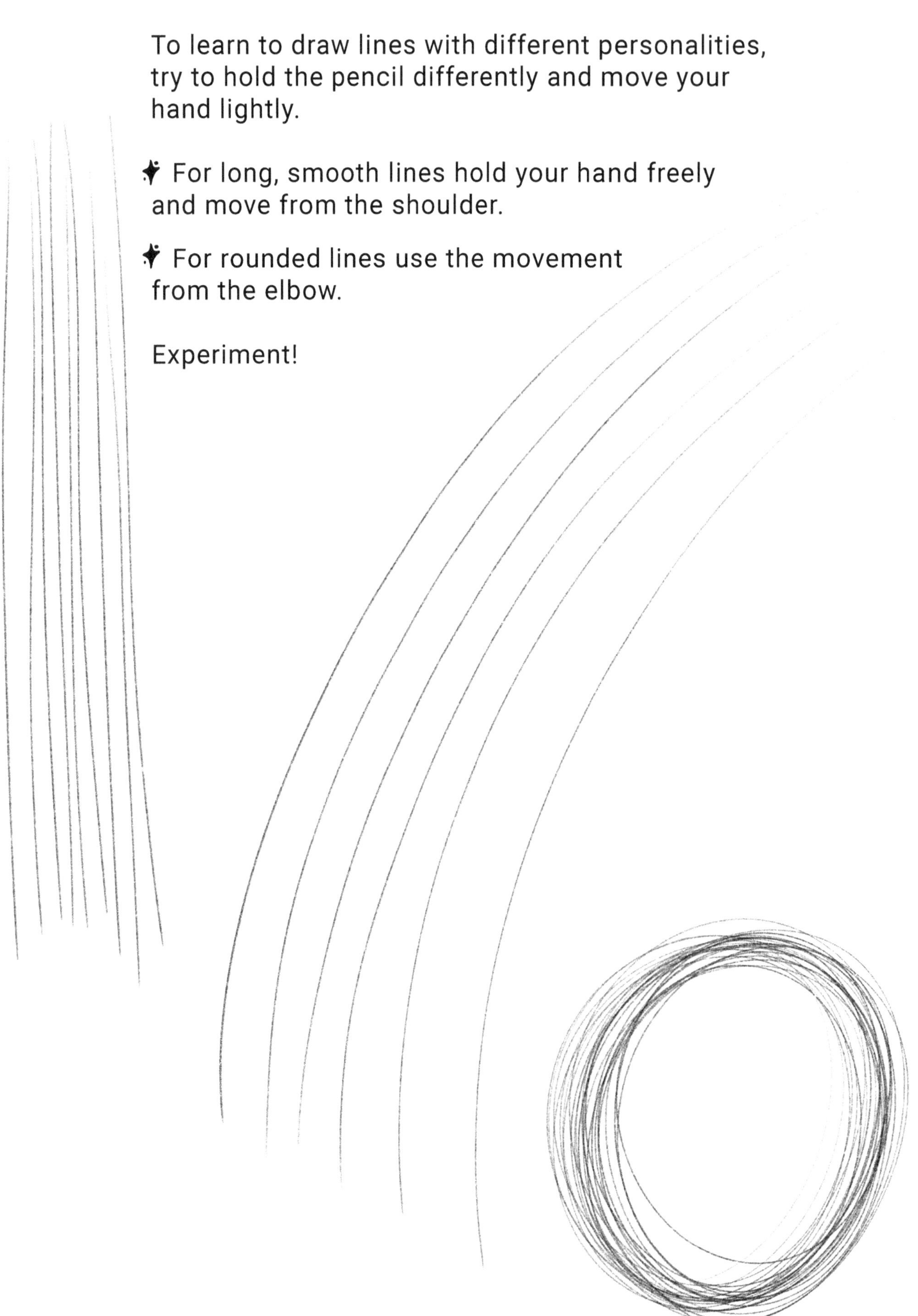

Try freehand drawing from your shoulder, holding the pencil lightly. Enjoy the beauty of the line!

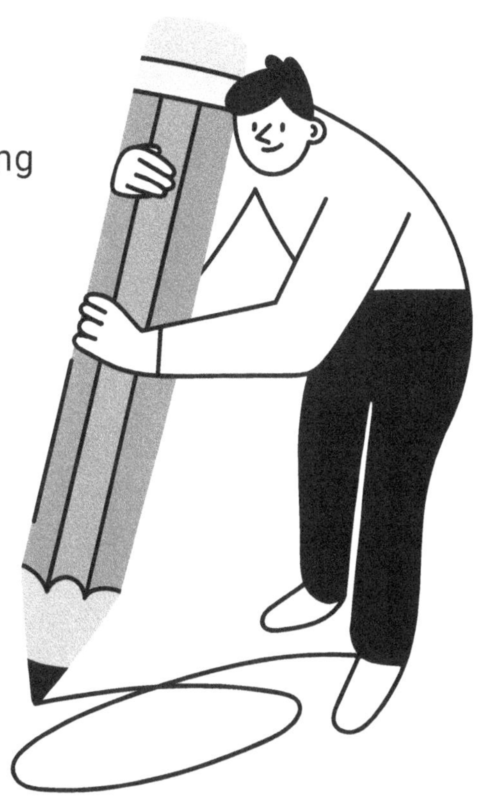

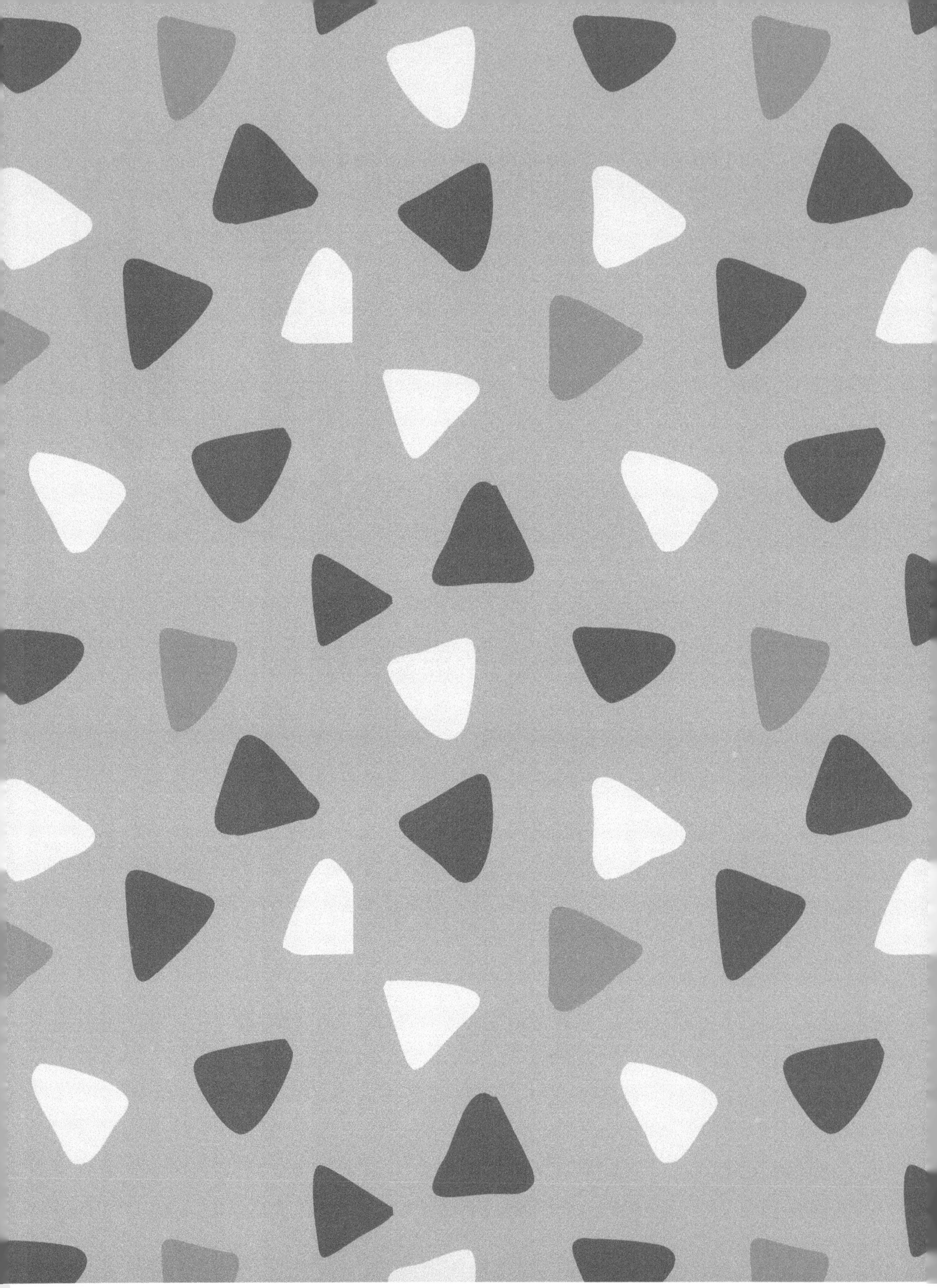

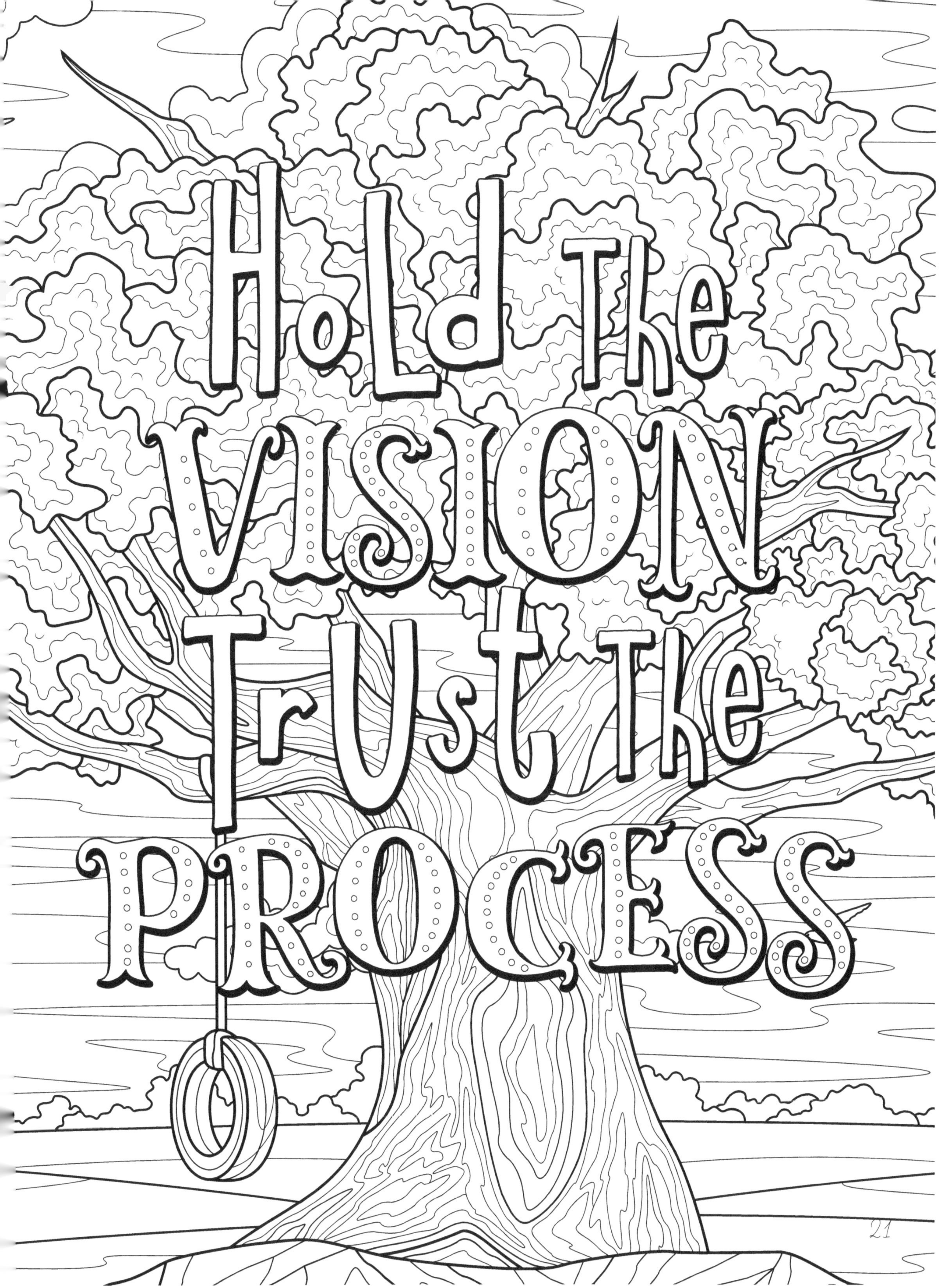

Hold the
vision
trust the
process

# BASICS OF LETTERING

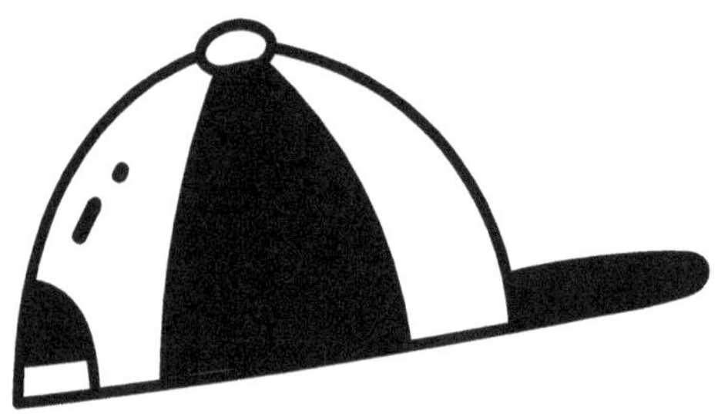 - color it

Beautiful writing requires time and concentration. Empowering yourself also requires time and focus: it doesn't happen overnight! When you learn calligraphy, you also sharpen your skills in concentration and attention to detail.

Using your familiarity with lines in the previous chapter, we'll start with some basic strokes. For this part, every down stroke should have heavy pressure. Push down on your pen or brush so that the lines come out thick. On the other hand, keep your hand light when drawing an upstroke. Upstrokes should be a thin line with less pressure on your pen. Go ahead and practice on this page.

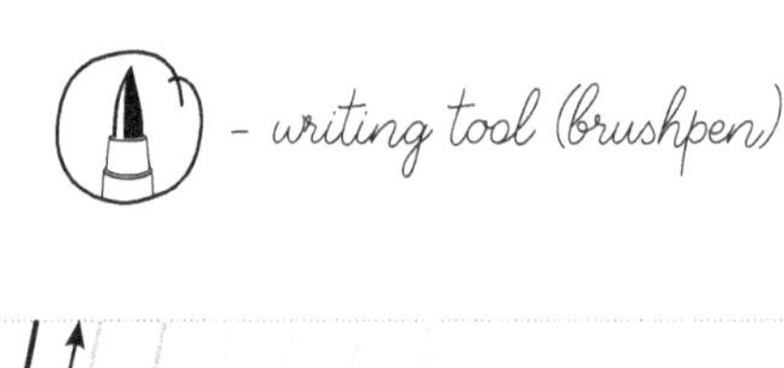 - writing tool (brushpen)

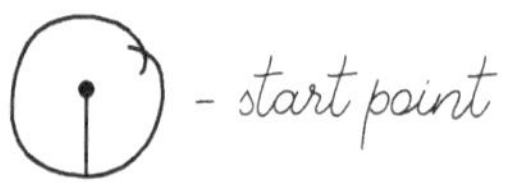 - start point

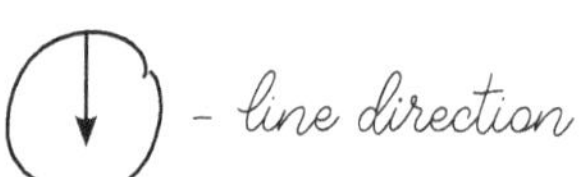 - line direction

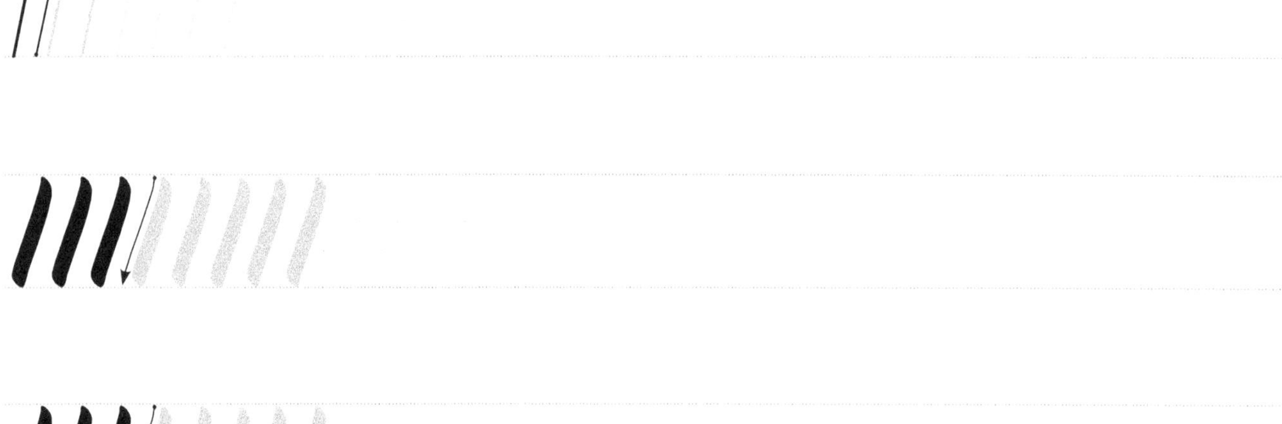



color it

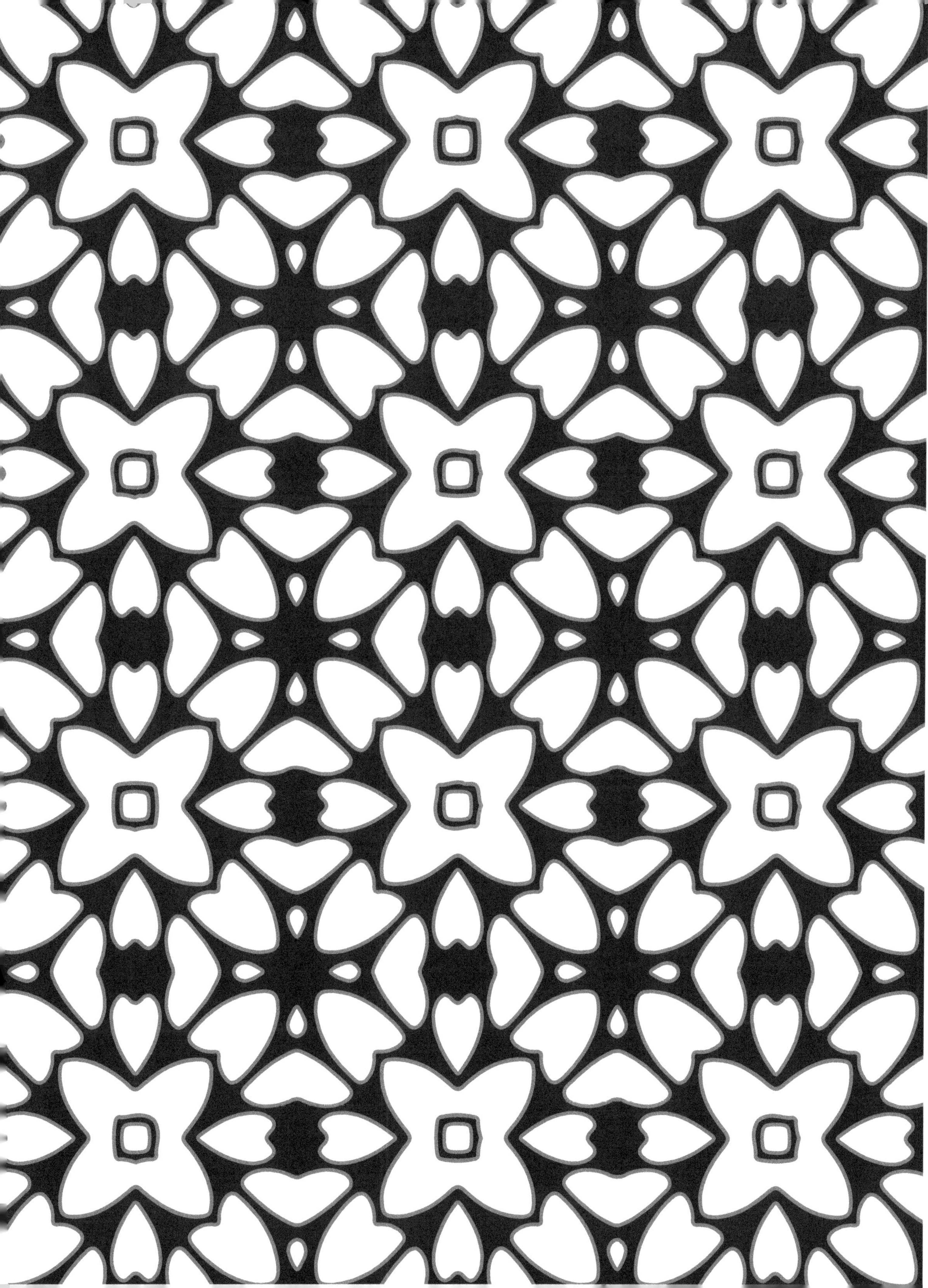

Now that you're getting the confidence to do the basic upstroke and down stroke, let's try connecting the lines with smooth transitions. Work on making the lines flow from thick to thin and without any sharp angles.

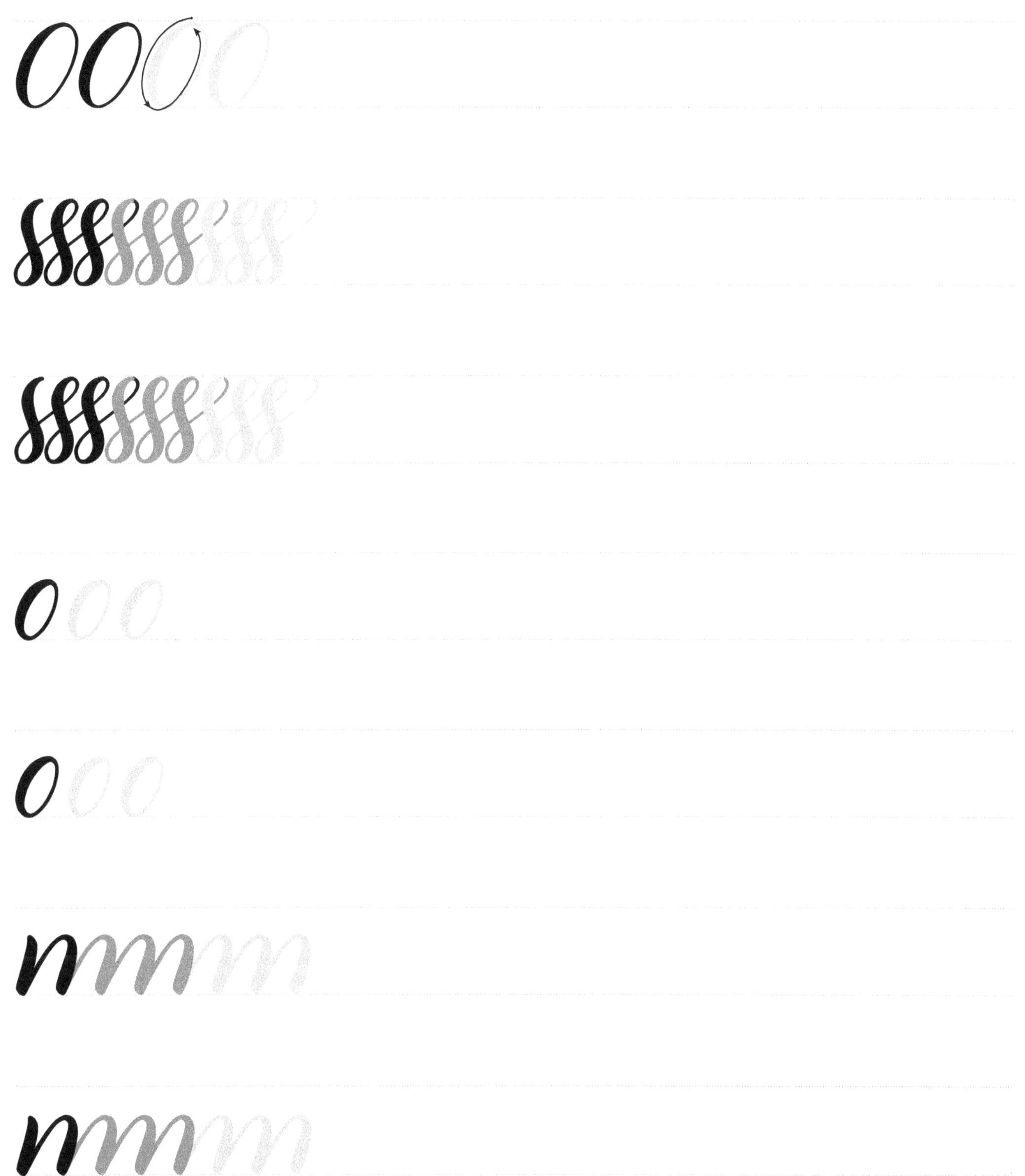

In lettering, as in life, learning the basics of any craft helps build strong foundations to create more complicated and beautiful works of art.

Living an intentional and empowered life grows with each decision to act, just as the flow of ink on paper marks each stroke.

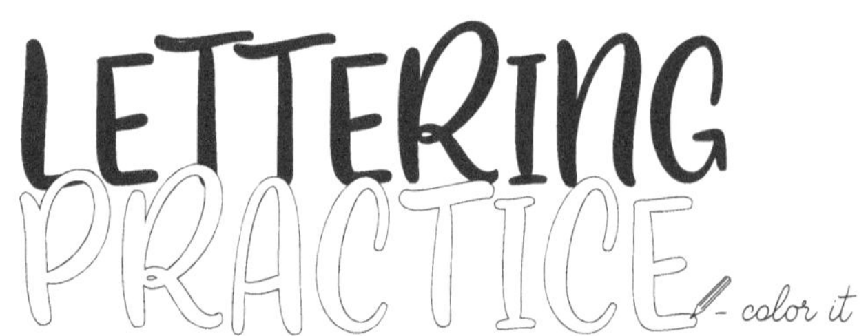



Emotions are highlighted when we are under pressure. How we respond to the pressure is our choice and can pave the way to an empowered future. In lettering, pressure produces clearer, darker lines.

Smoothly apply pressure as you move your hand down. Gently release pressure towards the end of the line and smoothly move to the next element. This script is bold but flexible. Try to convey the mood in the letters, as they have their own character!

✦ Follow the guidelines and use the blank space for practice

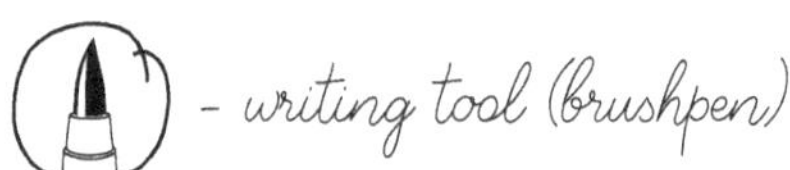


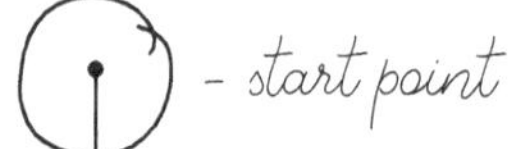


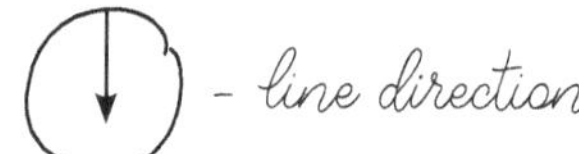


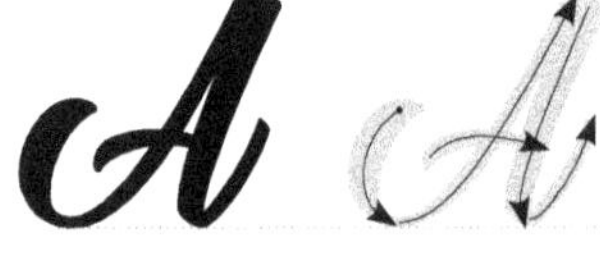

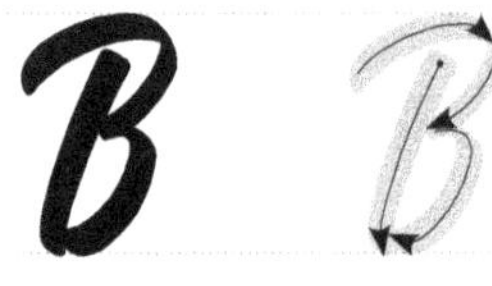

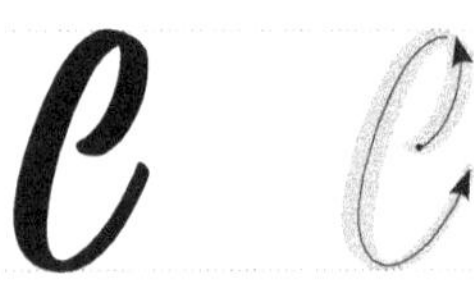

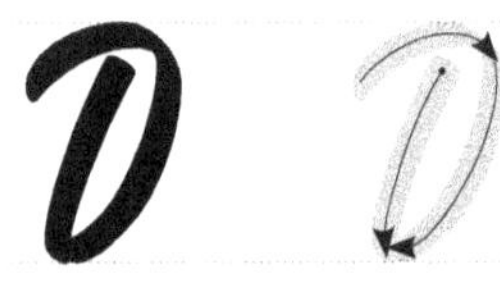

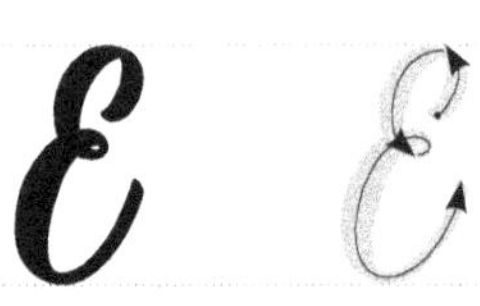

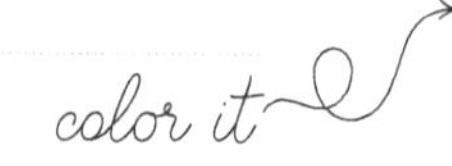

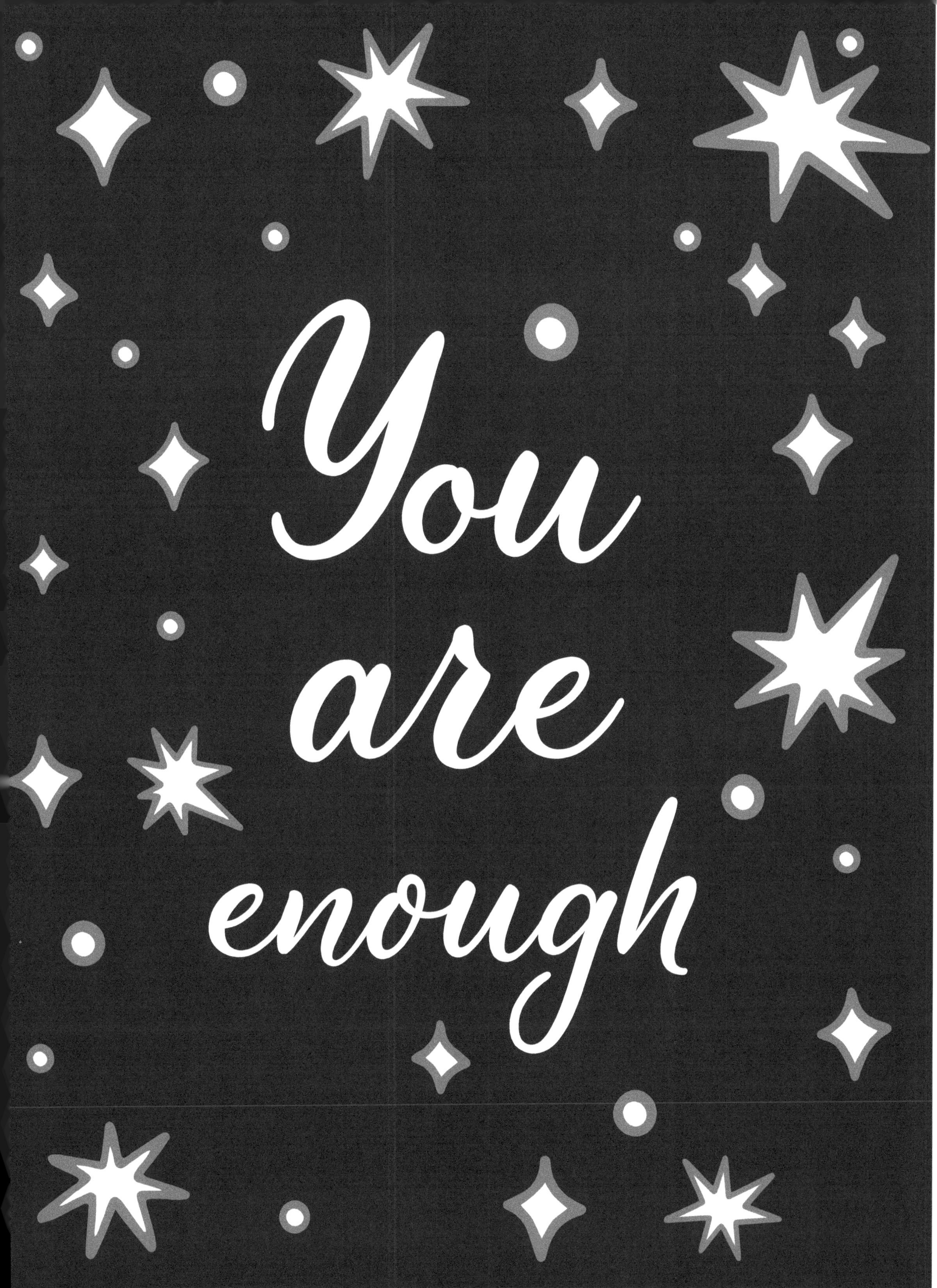

You
are
enough

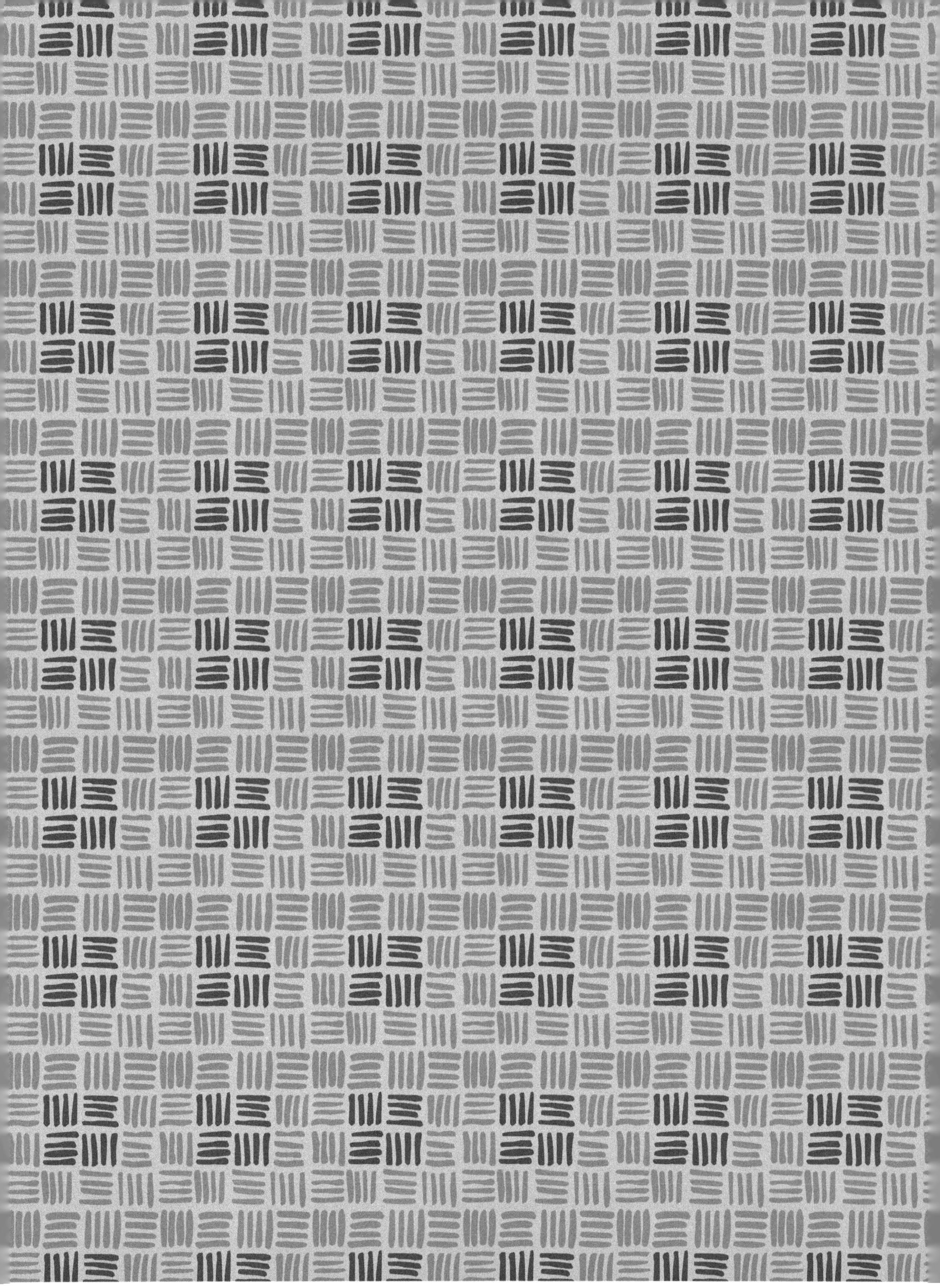

Each stroke becomes an expression of our innermost thoughts, a reflection of our inner power and strength. Our emotions find their way onto the canvas of paper, where they take shape and form, transforming into a tangible representation of our journey toward intentionality and self-confidence.

✦ Follow the guidelines and use the blank space for practice

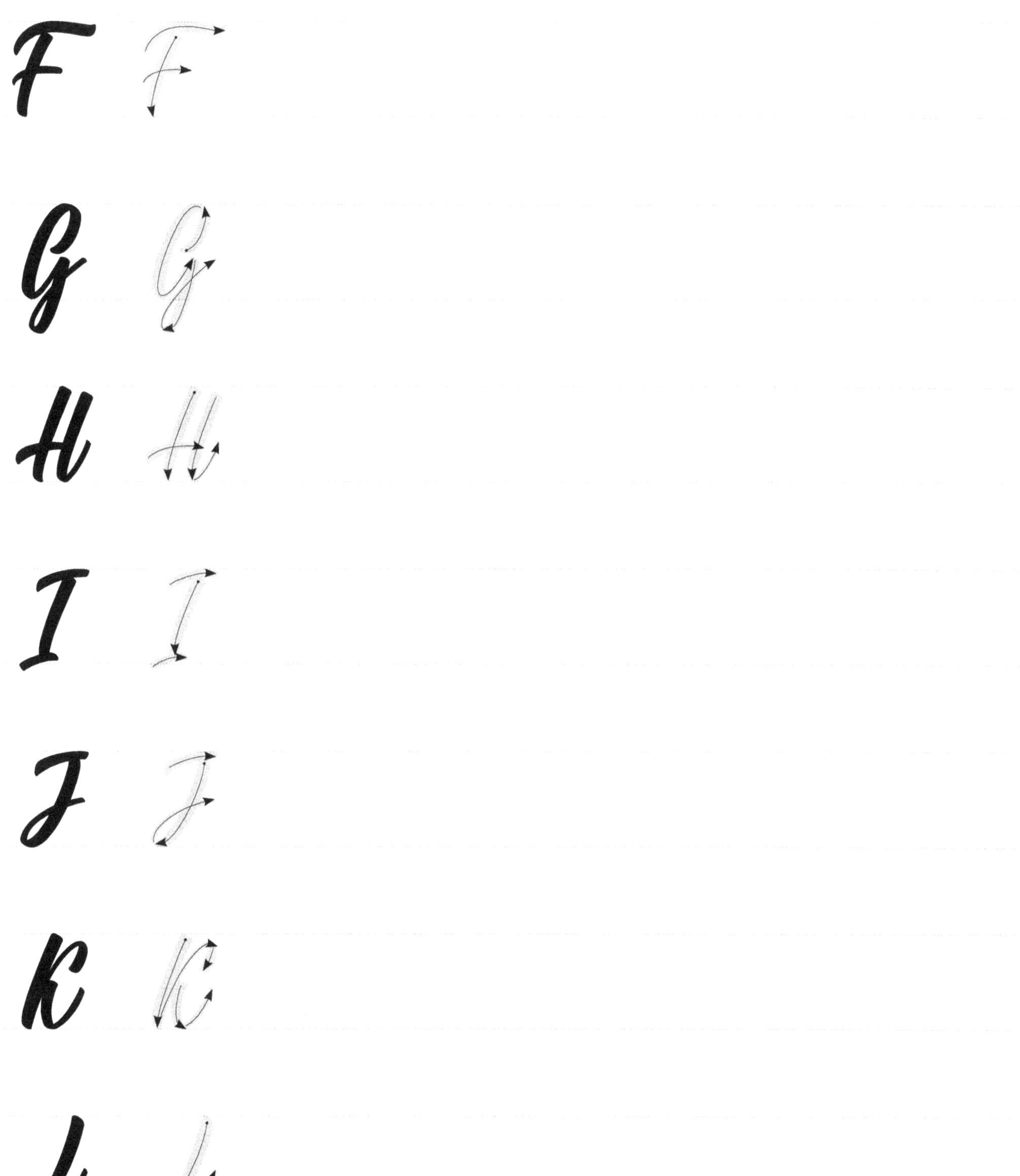

Giving yourself the opportunity to create, to make mistakes, and to improve on your skills is a great start to unleash a new and empowered you.

✦ Follow the guidelines and use the blank space for practice

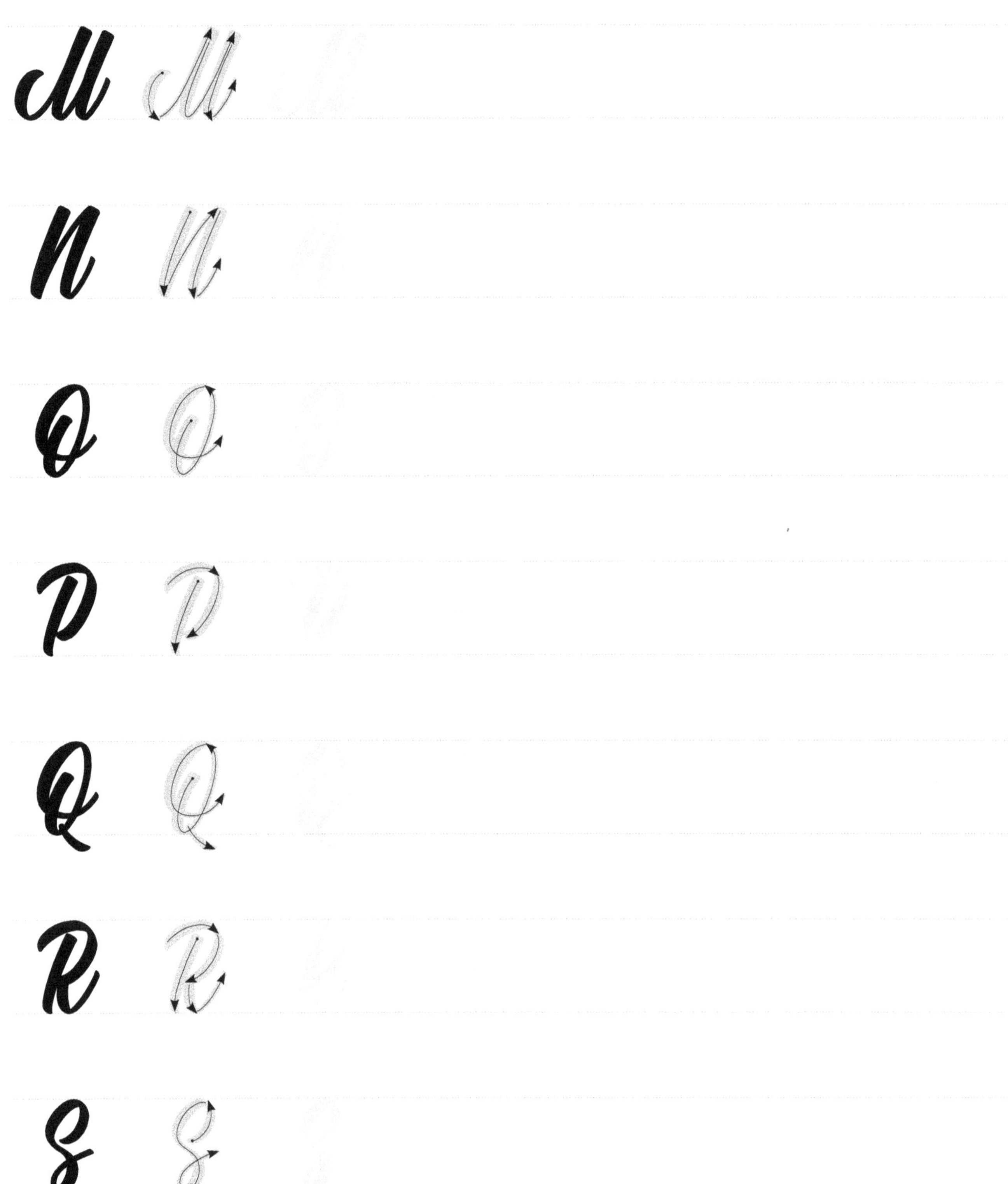

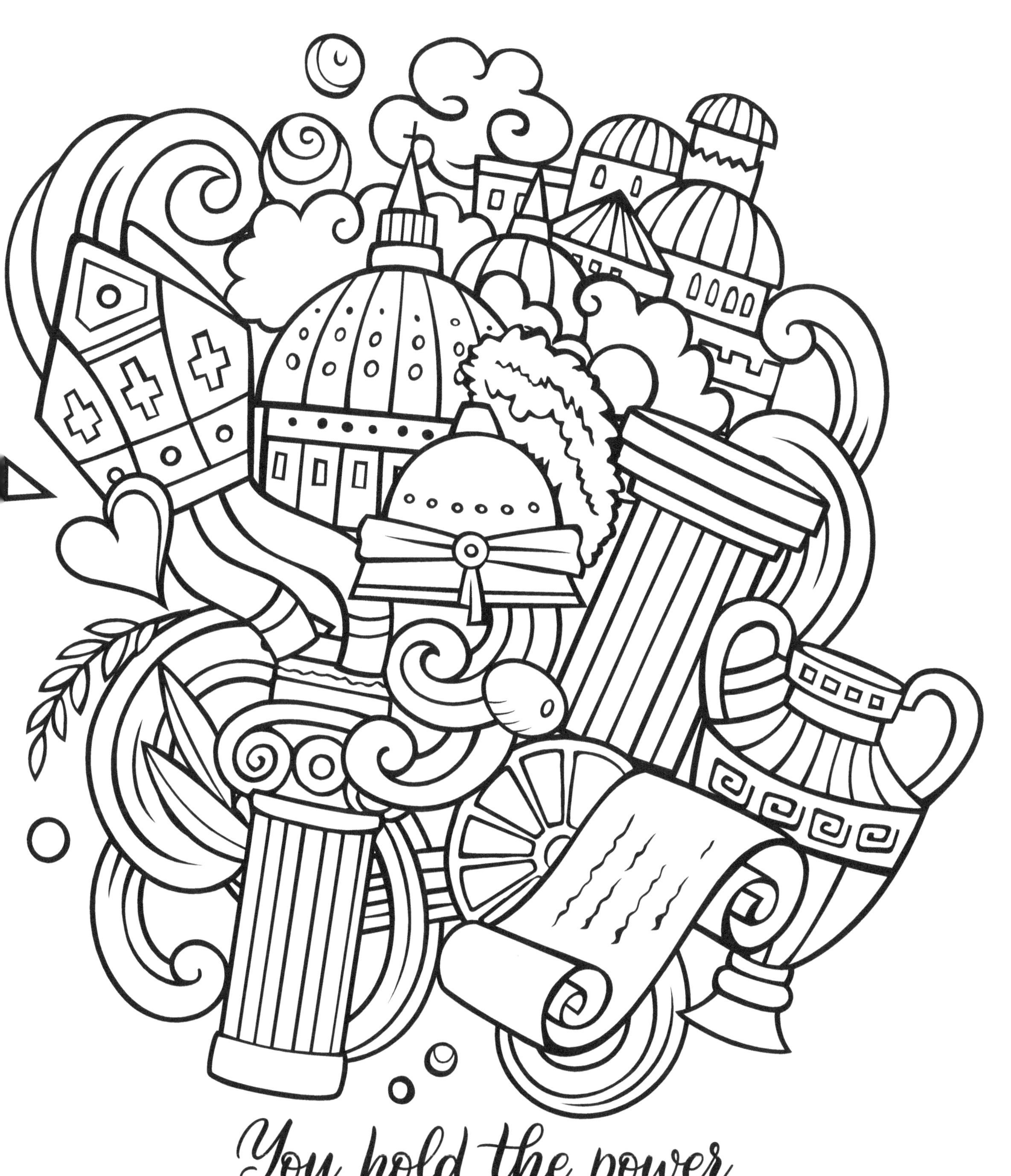

You hold the power
to shape your own destiny

Writing your thoughts using this lettering style can help in identifying areas in your life that need boldness and strength. What things do you want to do but still feel afraid to step out? Write them down with the letters that you have already practiced.

✦ Follow the guidelines and use the blank space for practice

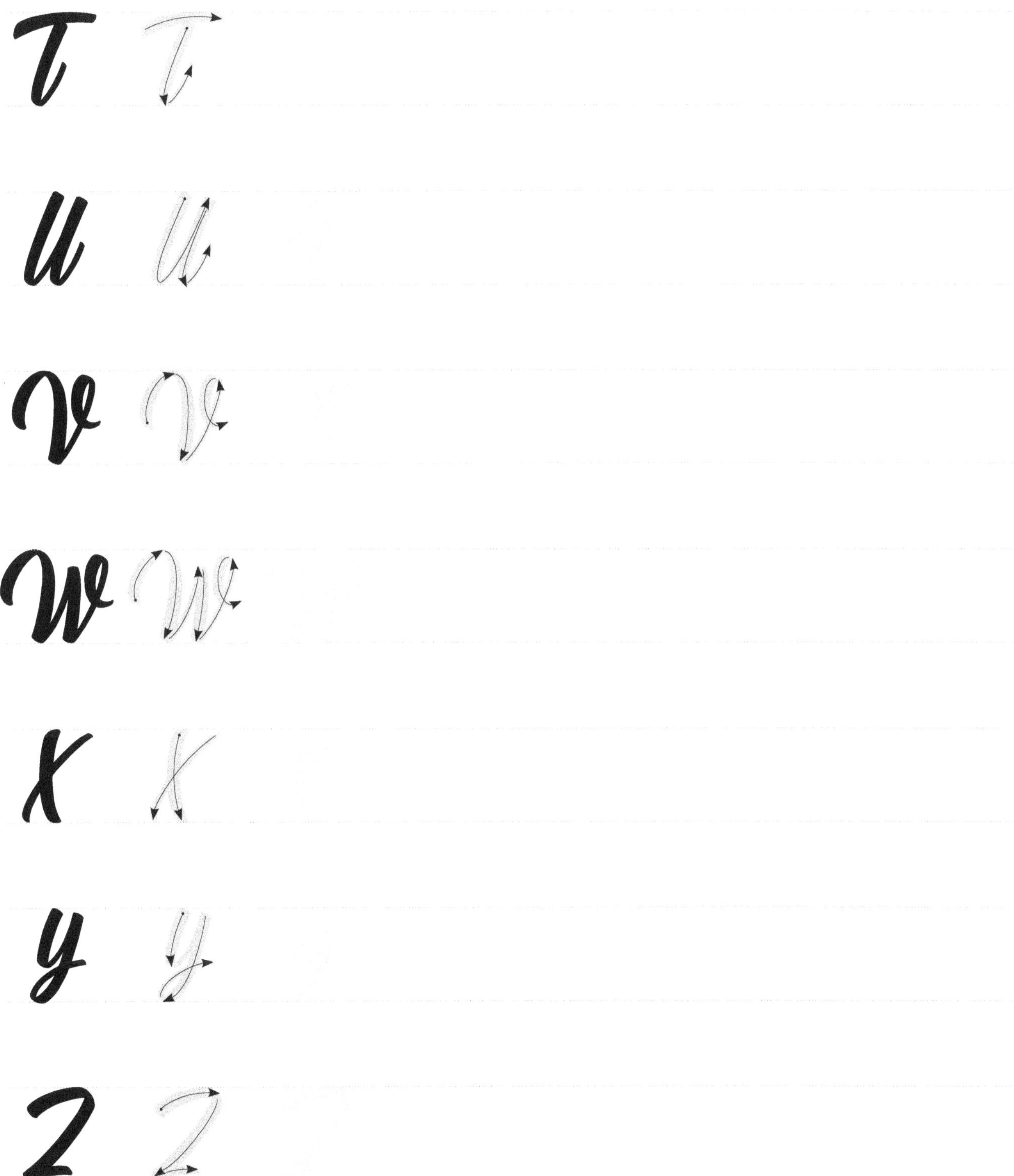

Once you feel comfortable writing in uppercase, you can now start practicing with lowercase letters. The adjustment you will experience in this practice will help in knowing that some things that are small in nature are still essential in life.

Switch from large to small shapes and practice the transitions with words that remind you to be strong.

*a a*

*b b*

*c c*

*d d*

*e e*

*f f*

*g g*

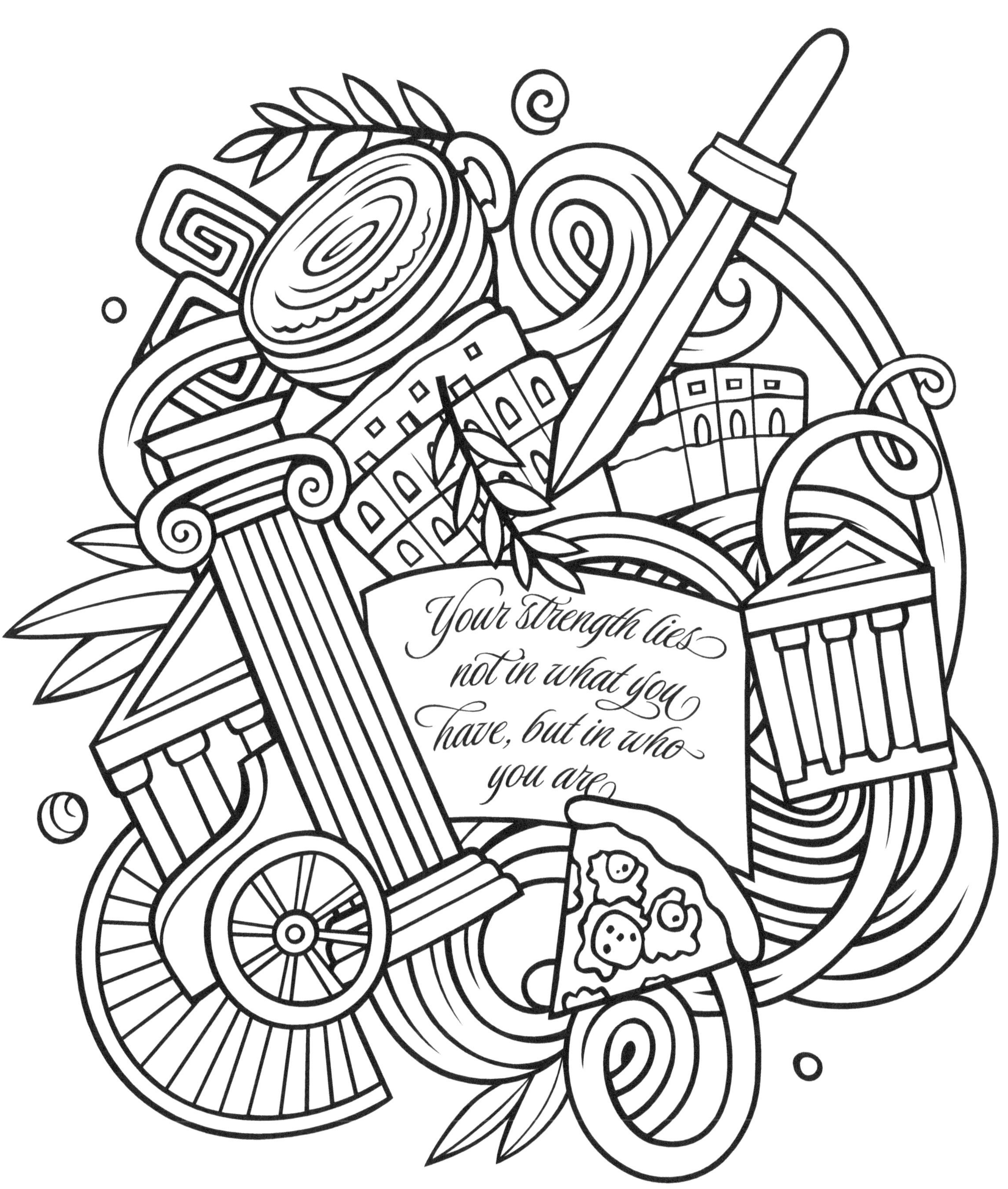

Your strength lies
not in what you
have, but in who
you are

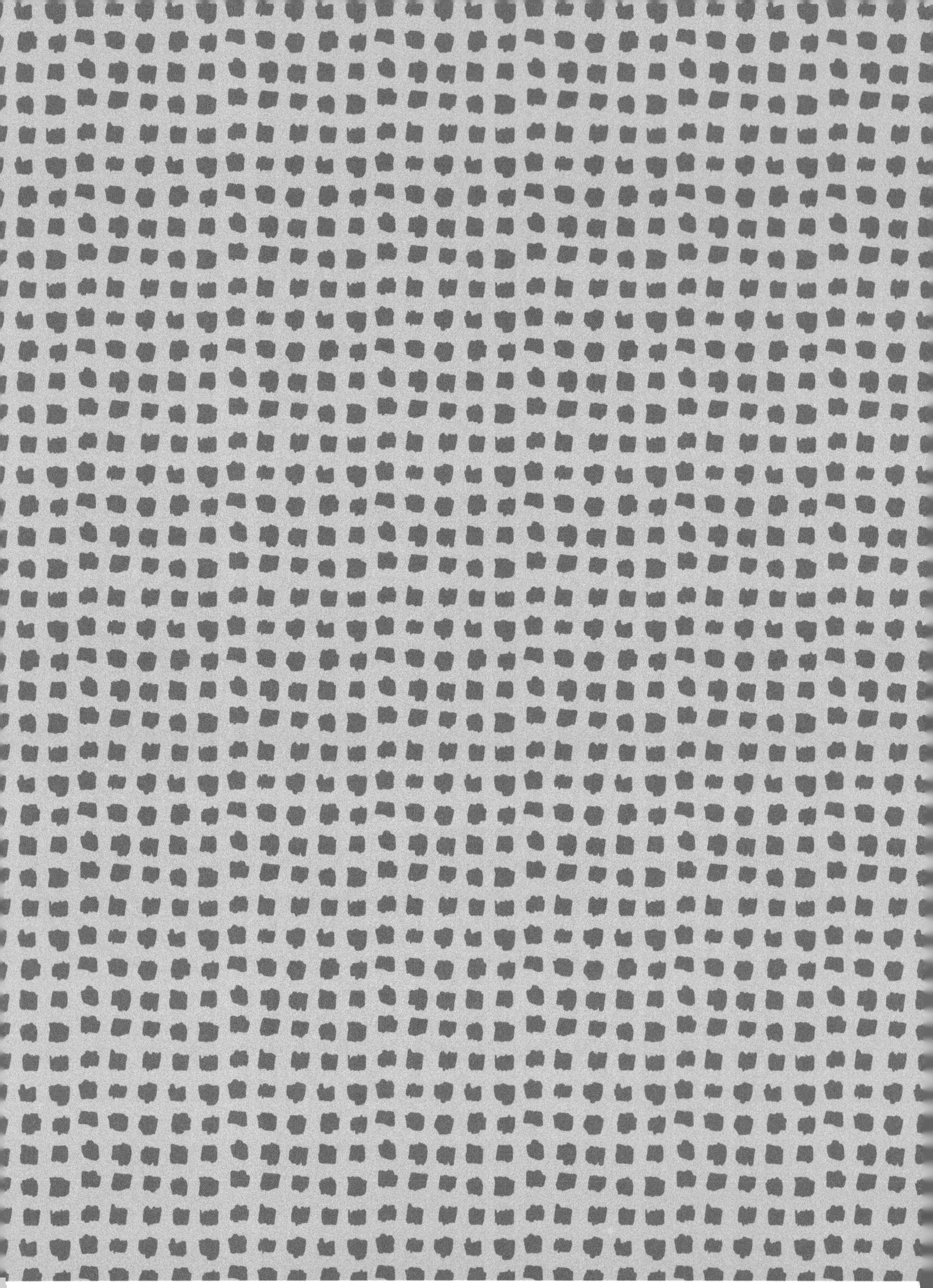

As you become more familiar with the strokes of the uppercase and lowercase letters, think about your power words. These are words you can say to yourself that make you feel strong. Reflect on these words for the next few exercises.

*h*

*i*

*j*

*k*

*l*

*m*

*n*

Being empowered does not only mean you can do whatever you want. It means you can do things and you also have the choice not to do them. Your choice is your power.

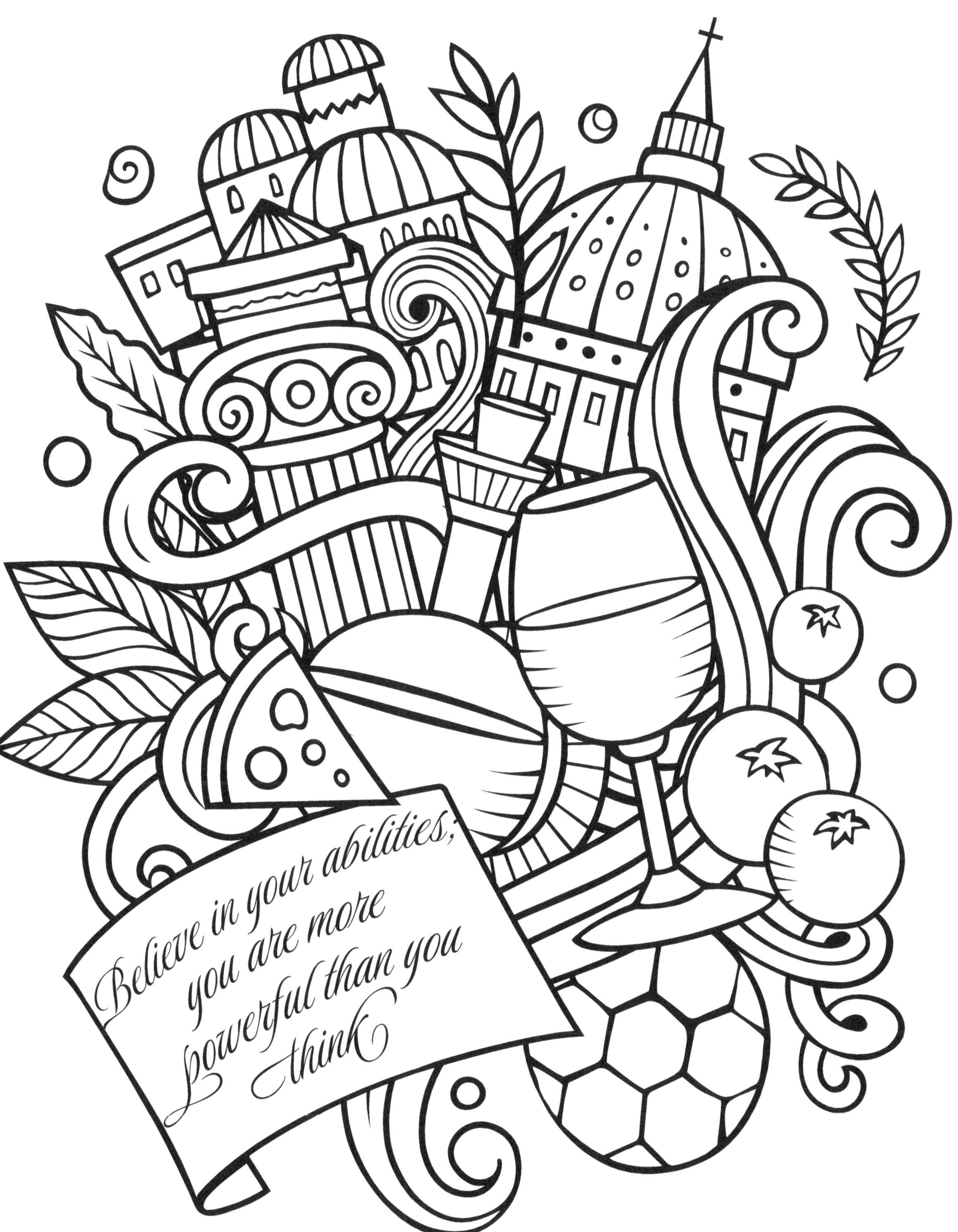
Believe in your abilities;
you are more
powerful than you
think

When you finish with the practices on this page, write down your chosen power words using the style you just learned. See how they match and what emotions they promote.

We will now practice a new style that adds more flourish to the letters.
Remember to use your basic strokes.

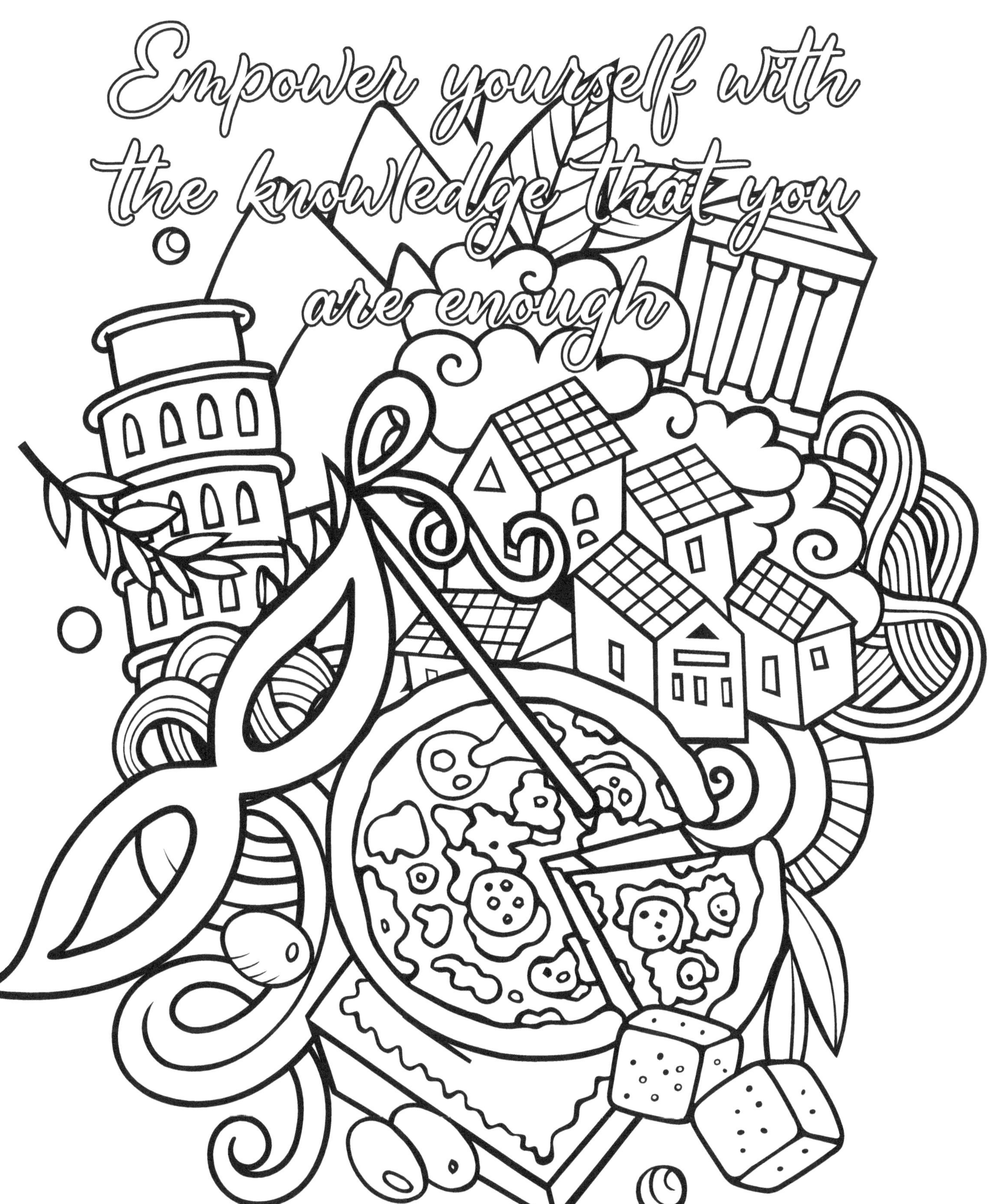

Empower yourself with
the knowledge that you
are enough

Your power lies within you. You may have been told the opposite for most of your life, but now you have to set yourself free. You can choose to do what is right and what is best for you. As you practice these letters, see yourself in this new light.

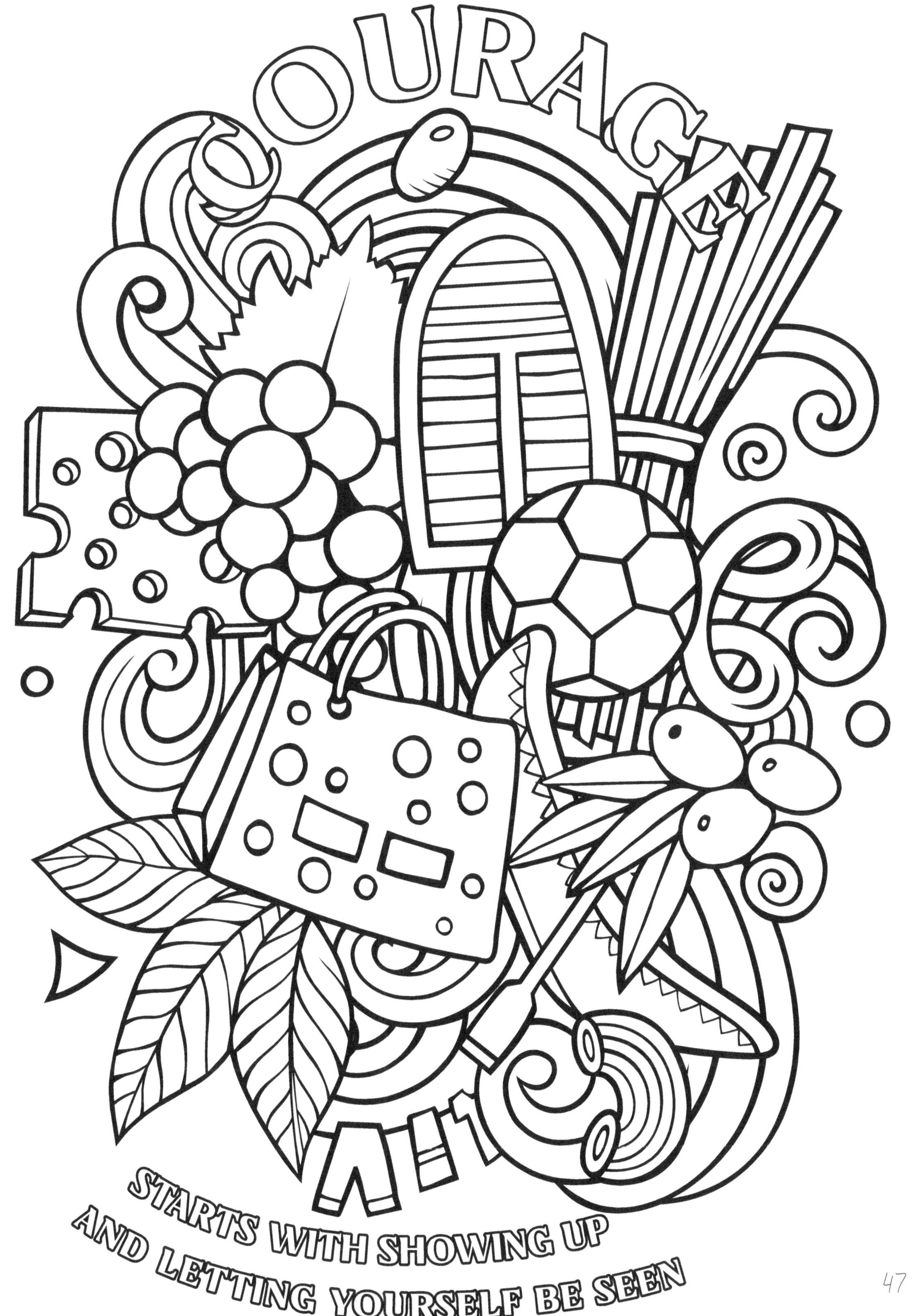
COURAGE
STARTS WITH SHOWING UP
AND LETTING YOURSELF BE SEEN

Repeating words and phrases help you retain the meaning. Practice writing these phrases and reflect on how they apply to you and your current situation.

*Believe you can and you're halfway there*

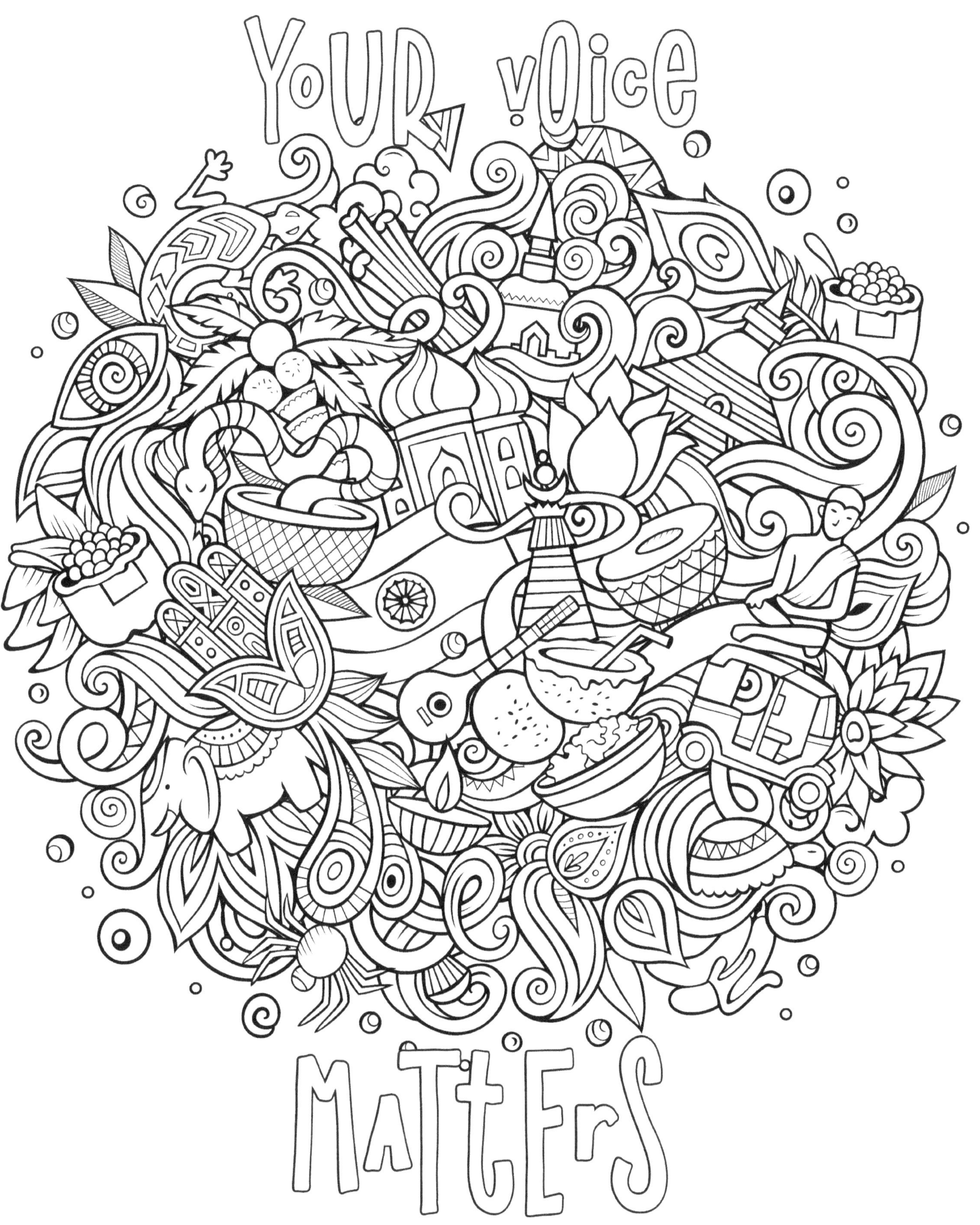

YOUR VOICE
MATTERS

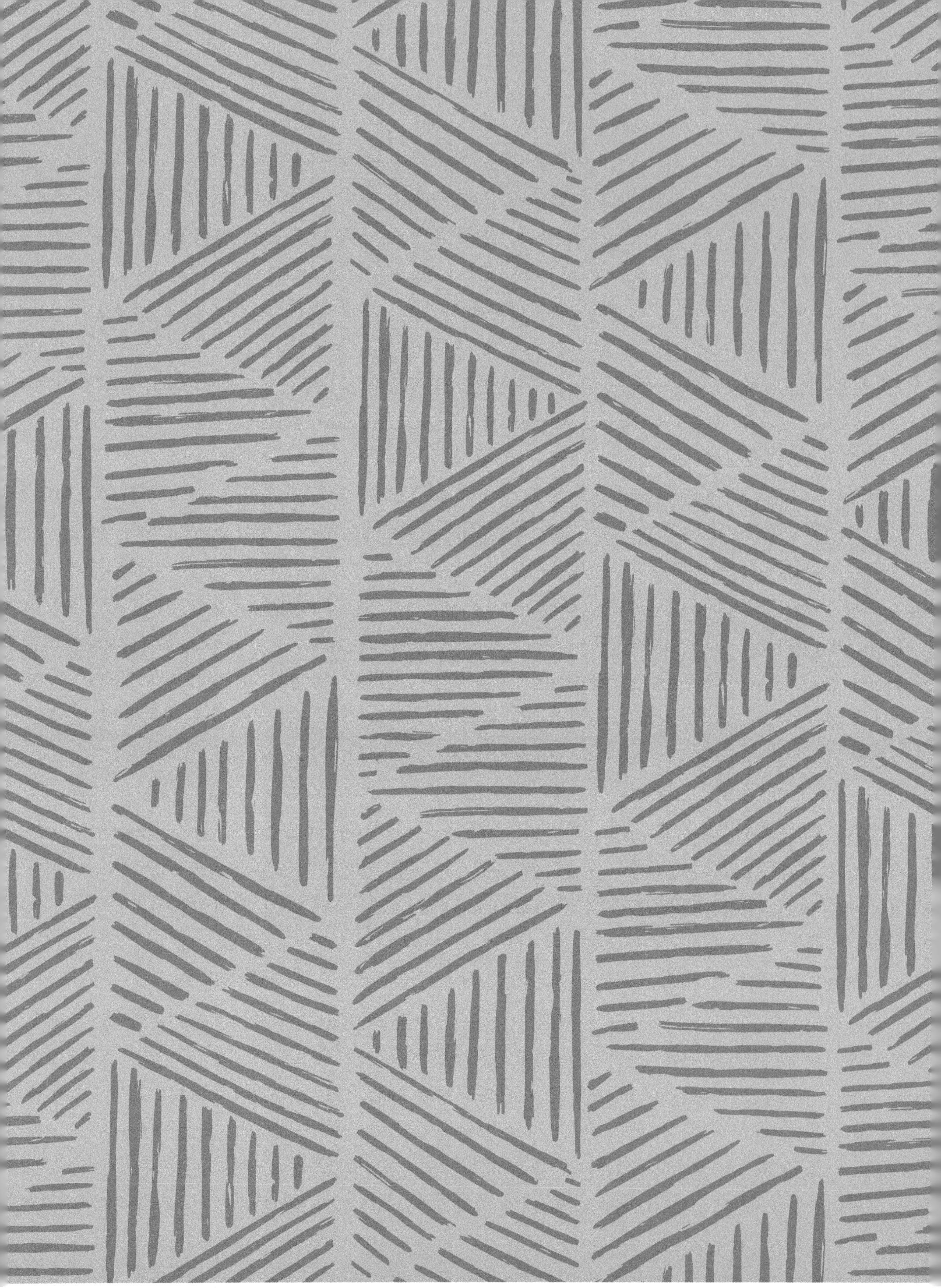

Authenticity and being yourself is an important part of self-empowerment. It shows that you are grateful for who you are and that you recognize the greatness that you can do.

Be yourself; everyone else is already taken

Now that you've mastered the more smooth and stylish font, practice on a new lettering style that's more direct. In this exercise, you will see both uppercase and lowercase letters, with some letters having options on how to write them.

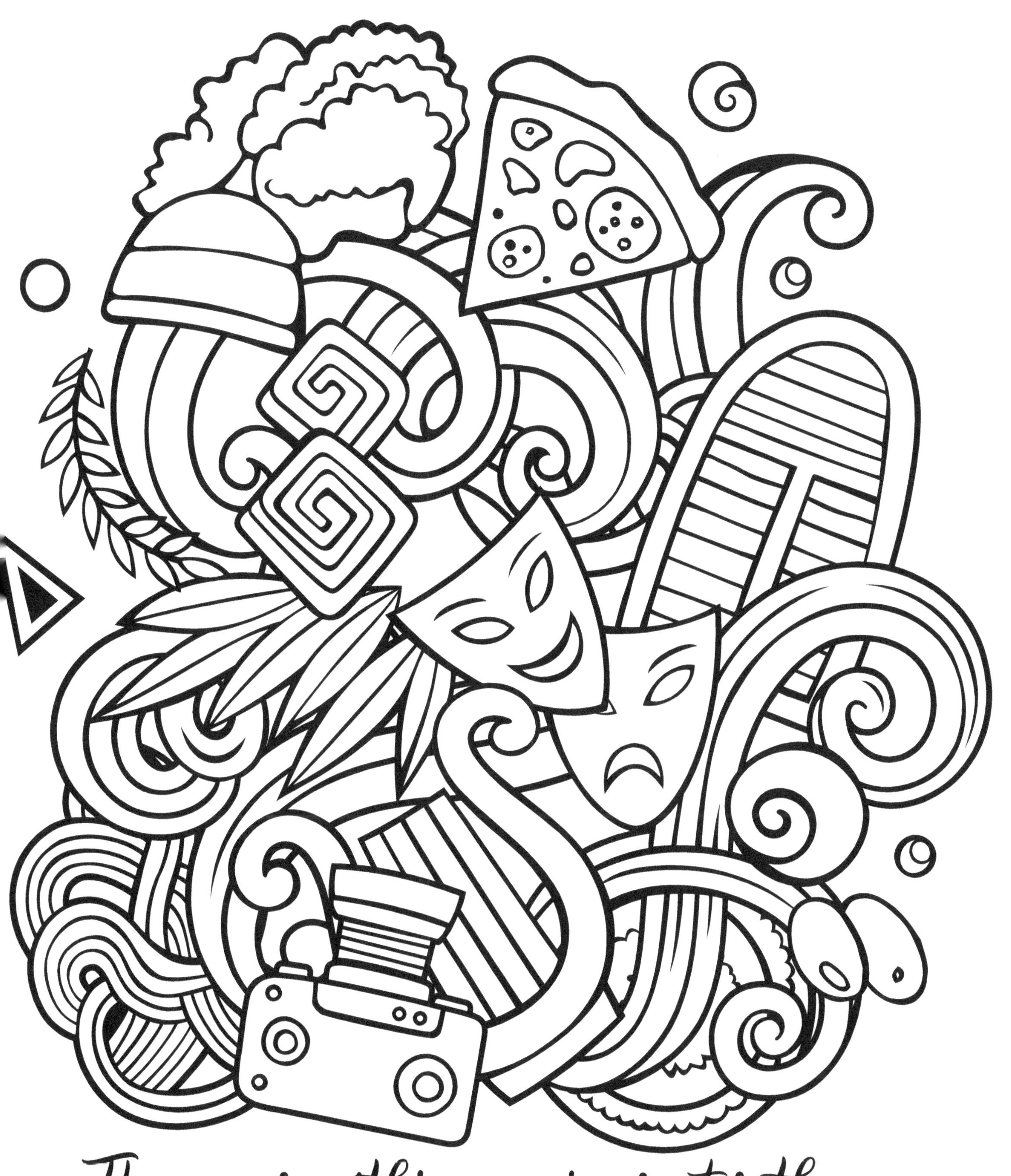

The power within you is greater than any obstacle ahead of you

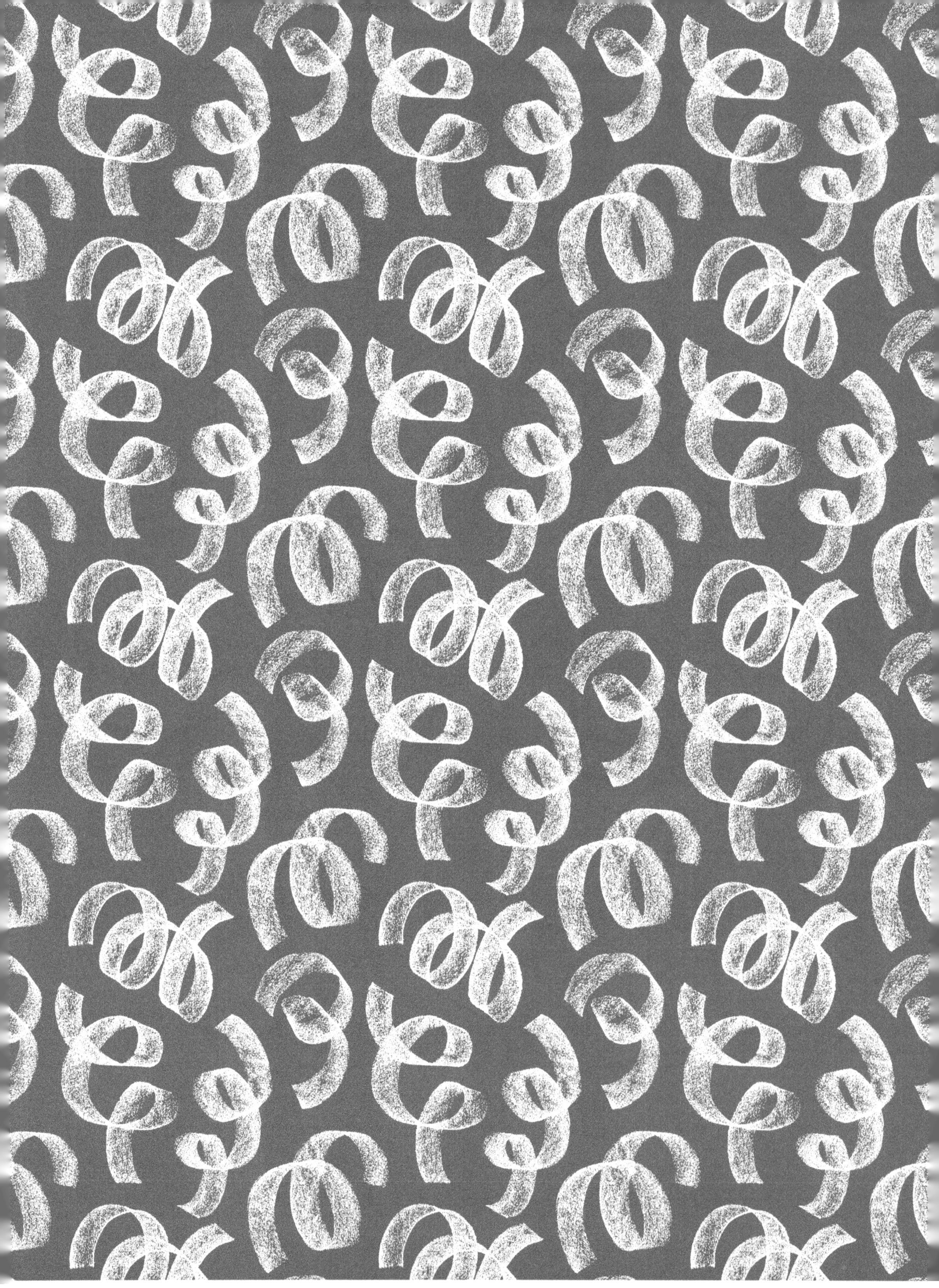

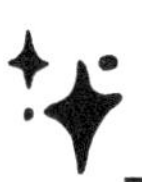

Though the exercises here seem simple, it takes control and focus to create and convey the type of message you want to put out into the world.

c c c

D D D

d d d

E E E

e e e

F F F

f f f

Think about the times when you empowered someone. Think about the words you used and how that affected the person. Now think about how you can write those words using the letters you are practicing now.

G G G G

g g g g

H H H H

h h h h

I I I I

i i i i

J J J J

Empowerment begins



when you decide
to be yourself

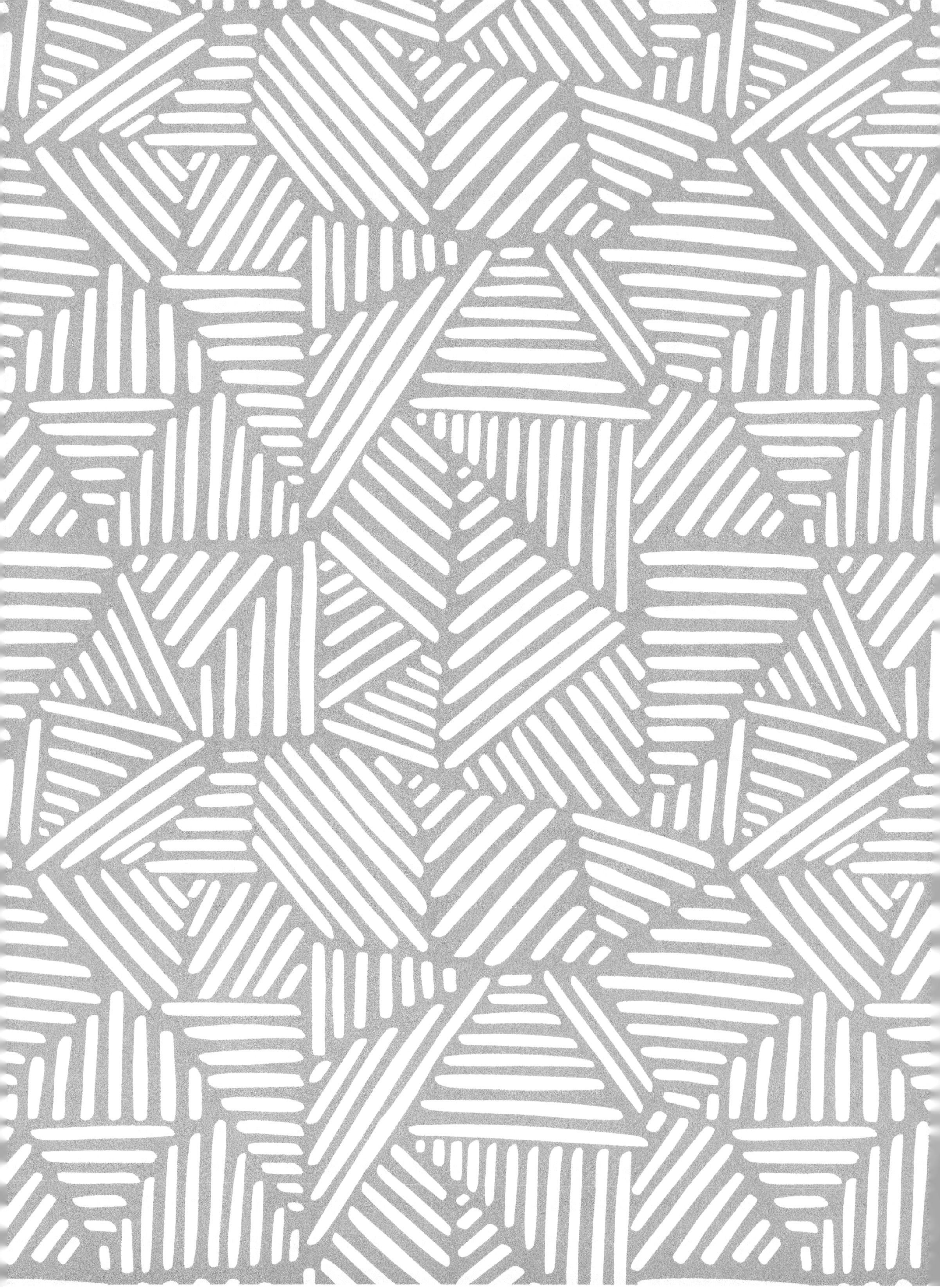

Each stroke you make must have a purpose. Each dot and line is created to convey meaning. Find the meaning to your message.

J J J

K K K

k k k

L L L

I I I

M M M

m m m

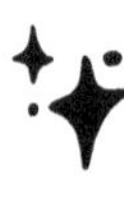 Take time now to rest for a while before continuing your exercises.
Breathe and find your focus. And when you're ready, start writing again.

N N N

n n n

O O O

o o o

P P P

P P P

Q Q Q

You have
the power to turn
your dreams
into reality

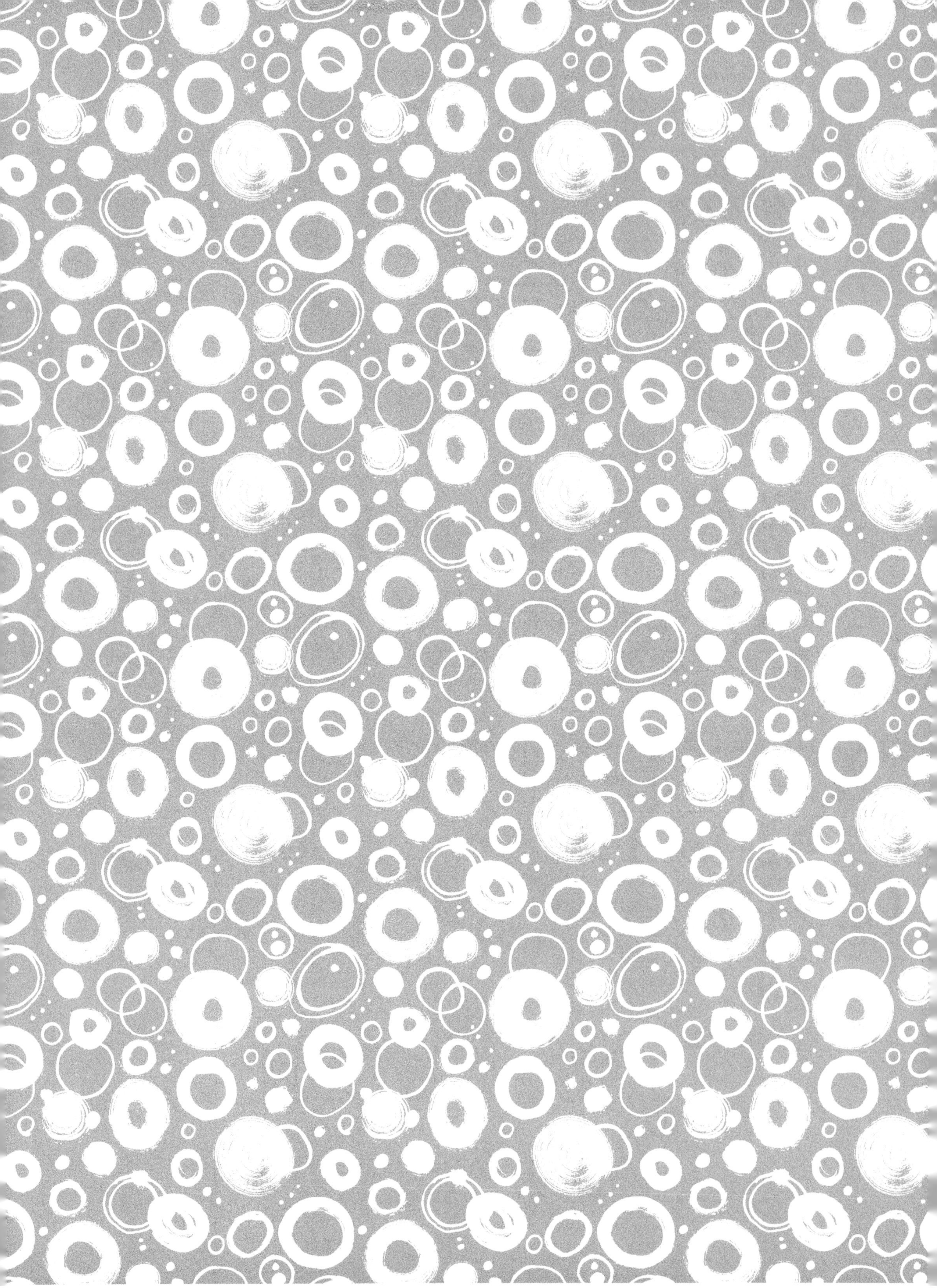

Have you ever thought of the many things you could have done if only you were brave enough to do them? You have the choice and the power to make changes in your life. The best time to start taking the necessary steps is now.

Empowerment takes a lot of courage. You need to find your *why* and stick to the process, much like how you've been practicing these letter styles.

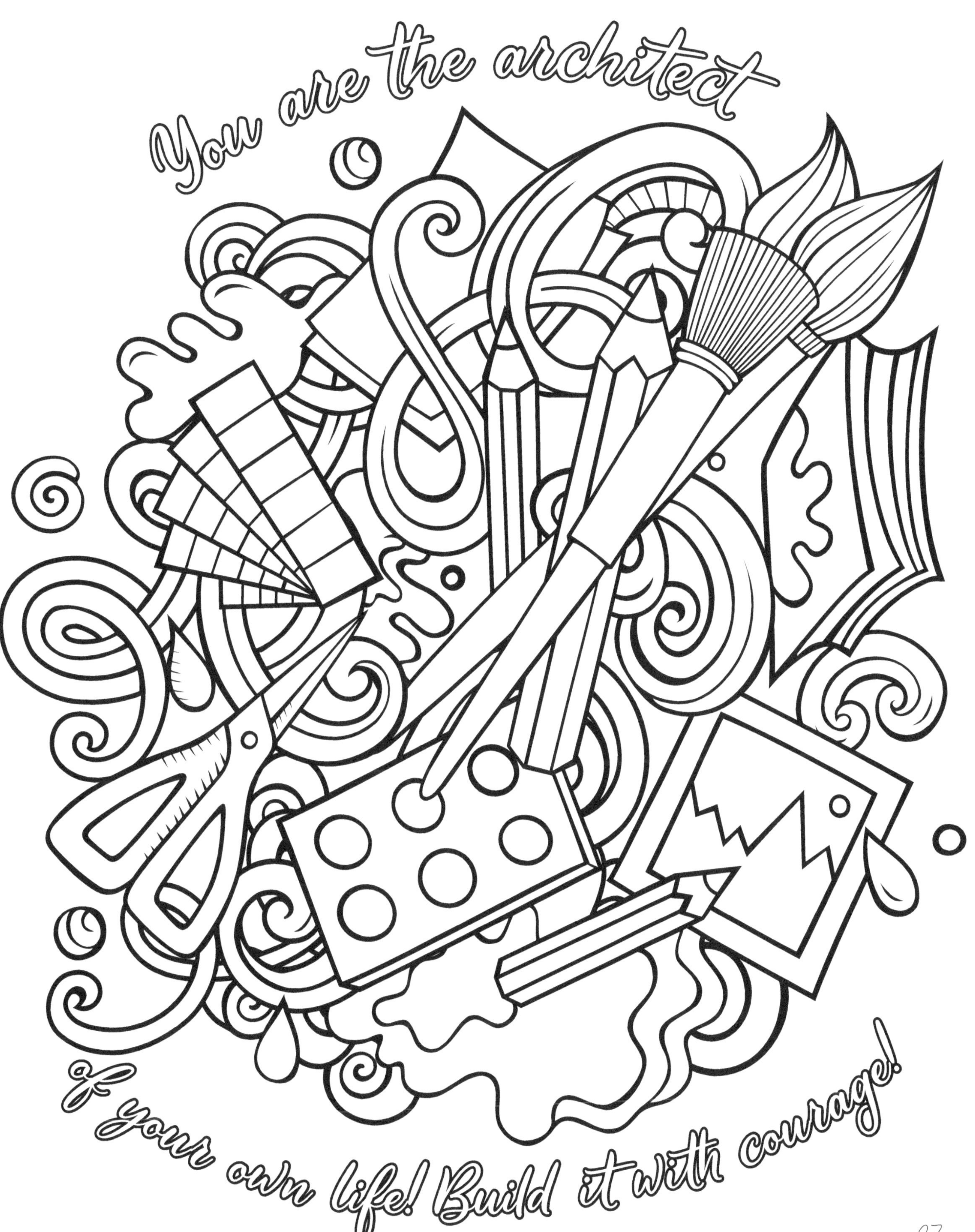

You are the architect
of your own life! Build it with courage!

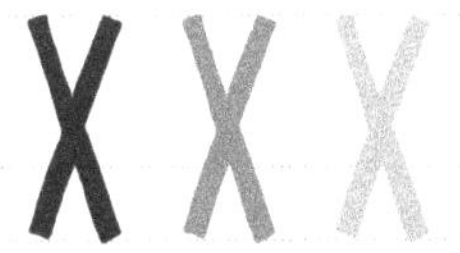

Remember to celebrate your wins no matter how small. For example, you've successfully practiced three lettering styles and you should be so proud of yourself. Congratulations!

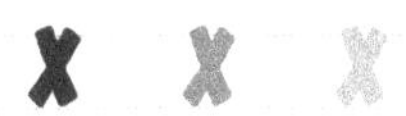

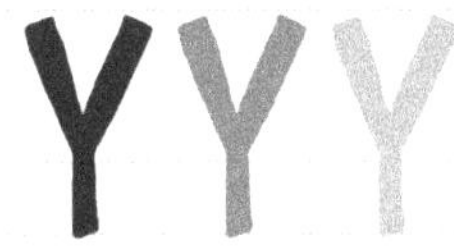

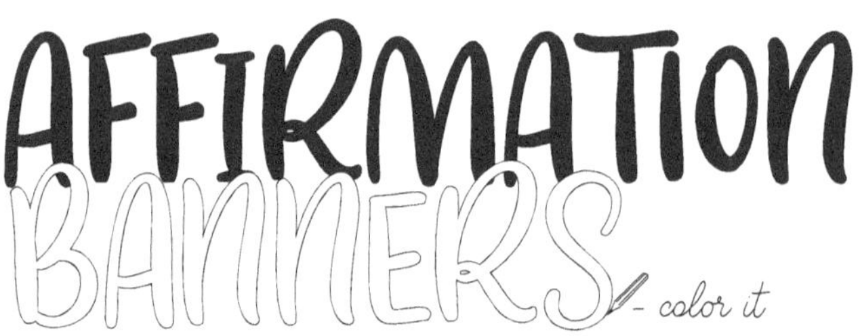


A big part of empowerment is positive affirmation. What you tell yourself and what other people say to you affects the way you perceive yourself whether you notice it or not.

For the next few pages, find a place where you can focus and reflect on who you are and who you want to be. After a few minutes, list down the words that describe you. Use what you learned in the previous pages and creatively write affirmations on the banners prepared on the pages.

The affirmations will not only describe who you are now but who you also want to be. Empower yourself through the lettering styles you have mastered.

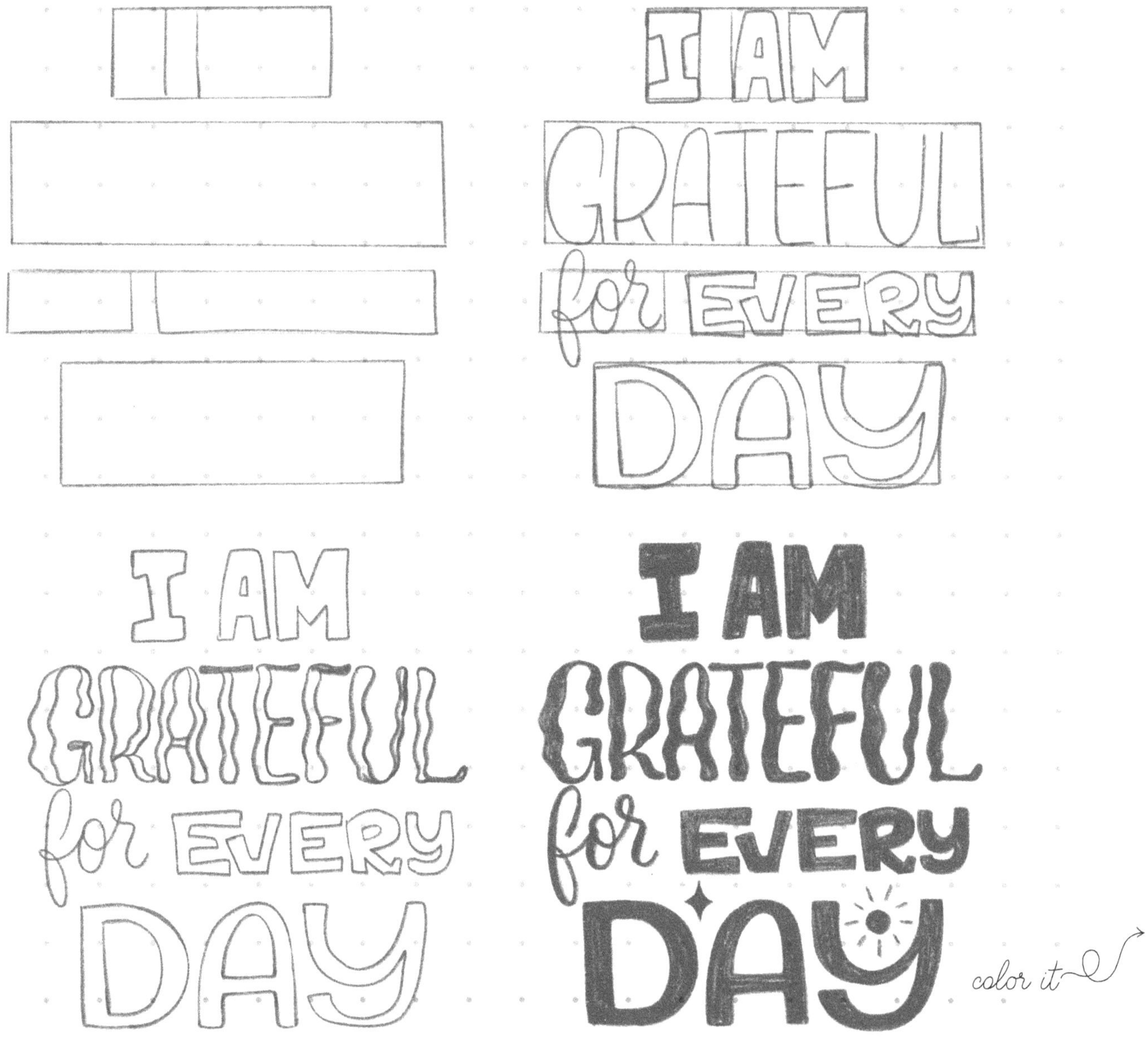

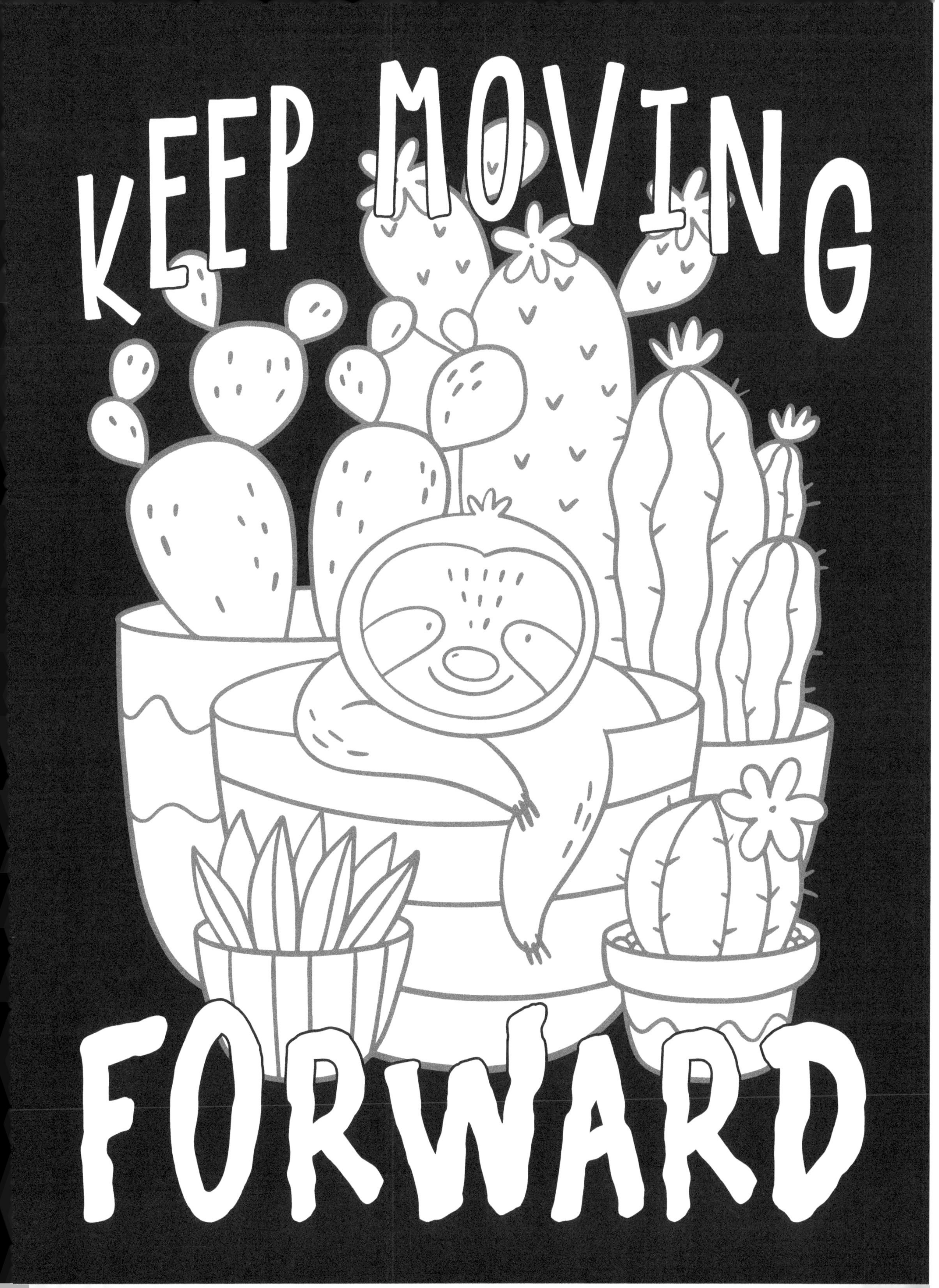

KEEP MOVING
FORWARD

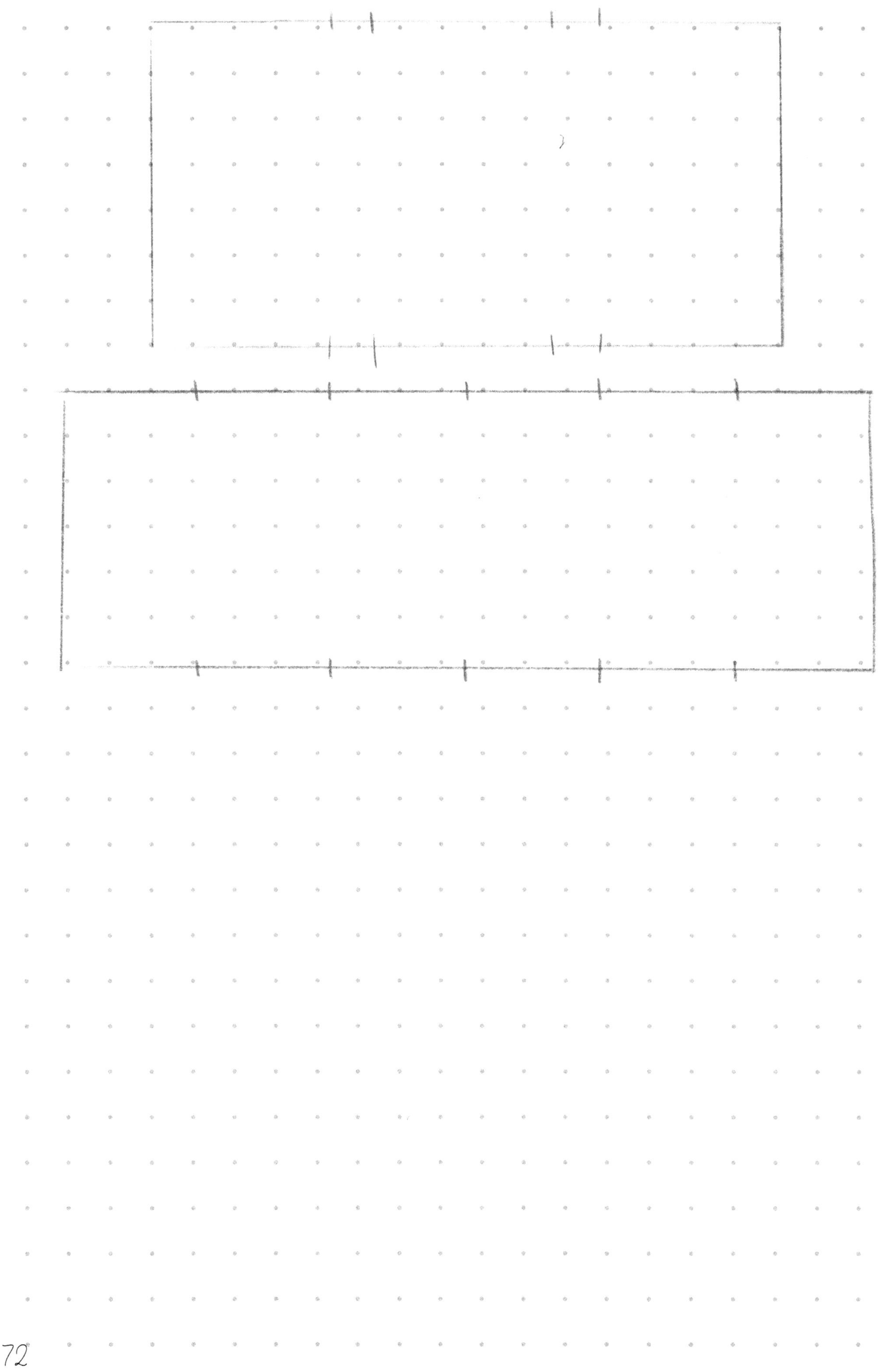

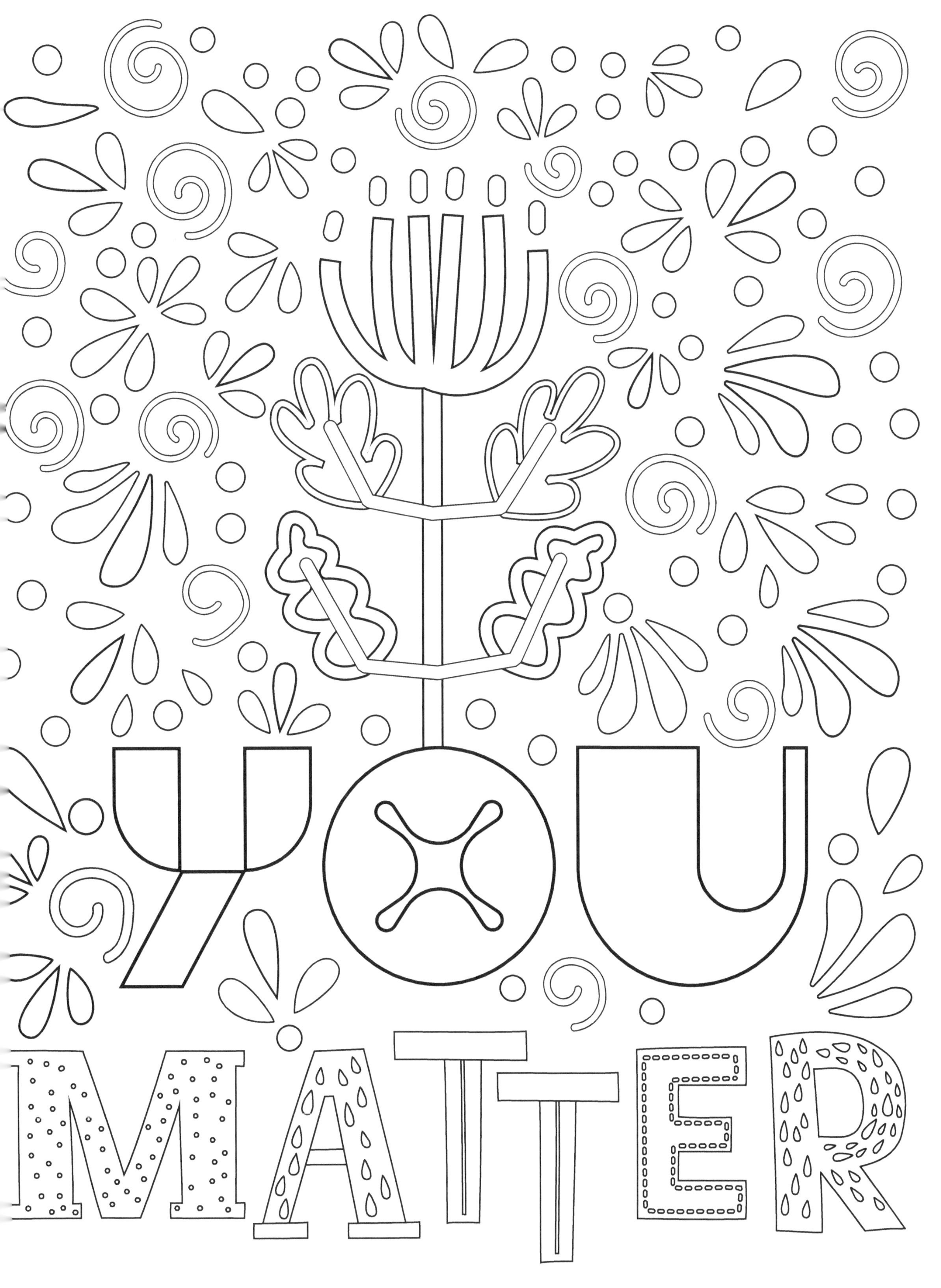

YOU
MATTER

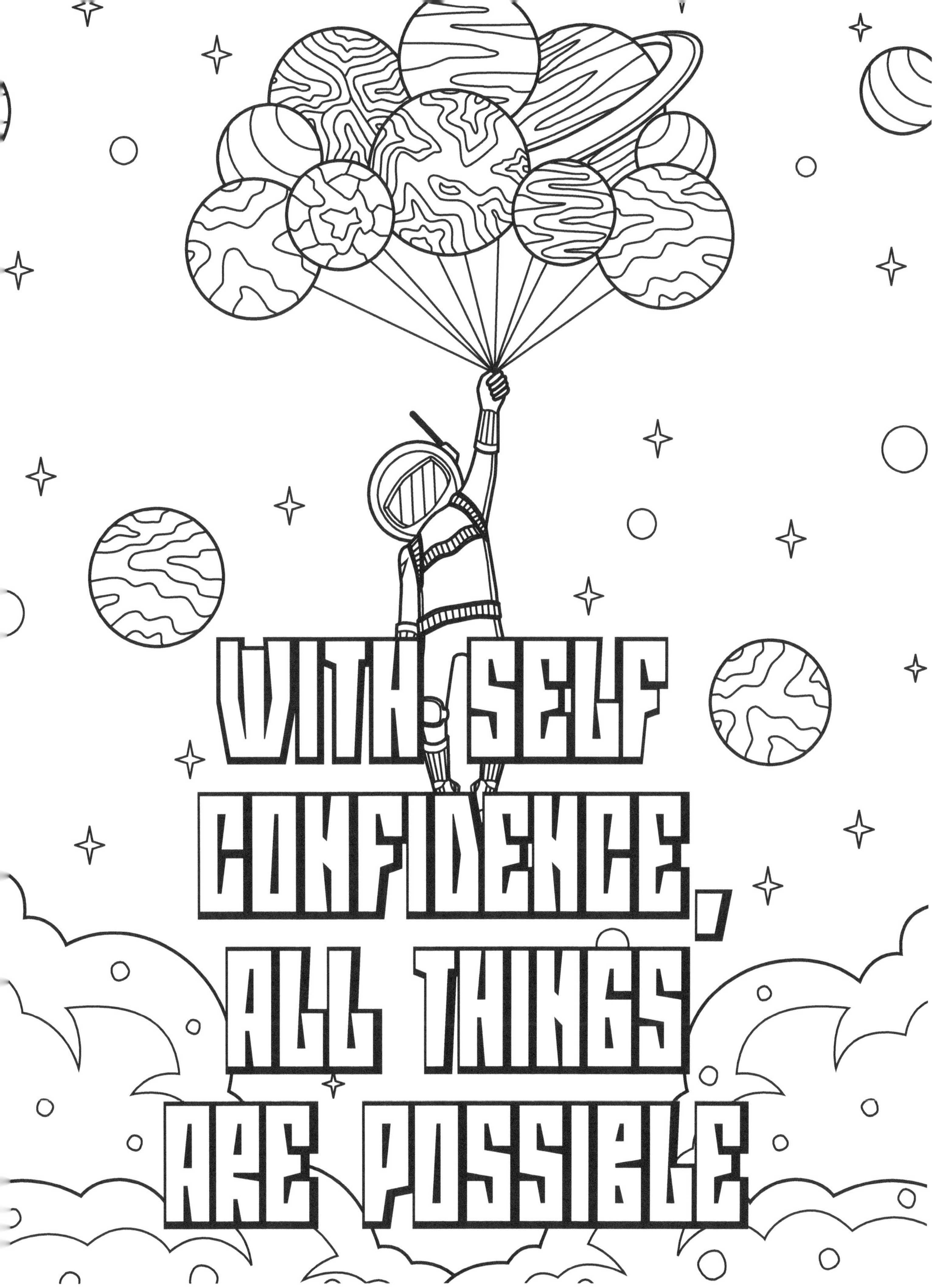

WITH SELF CONFIDENCE, ALL THINGS ARE POSSIBLE

TRAIN
LIKE
A
CHAMPION

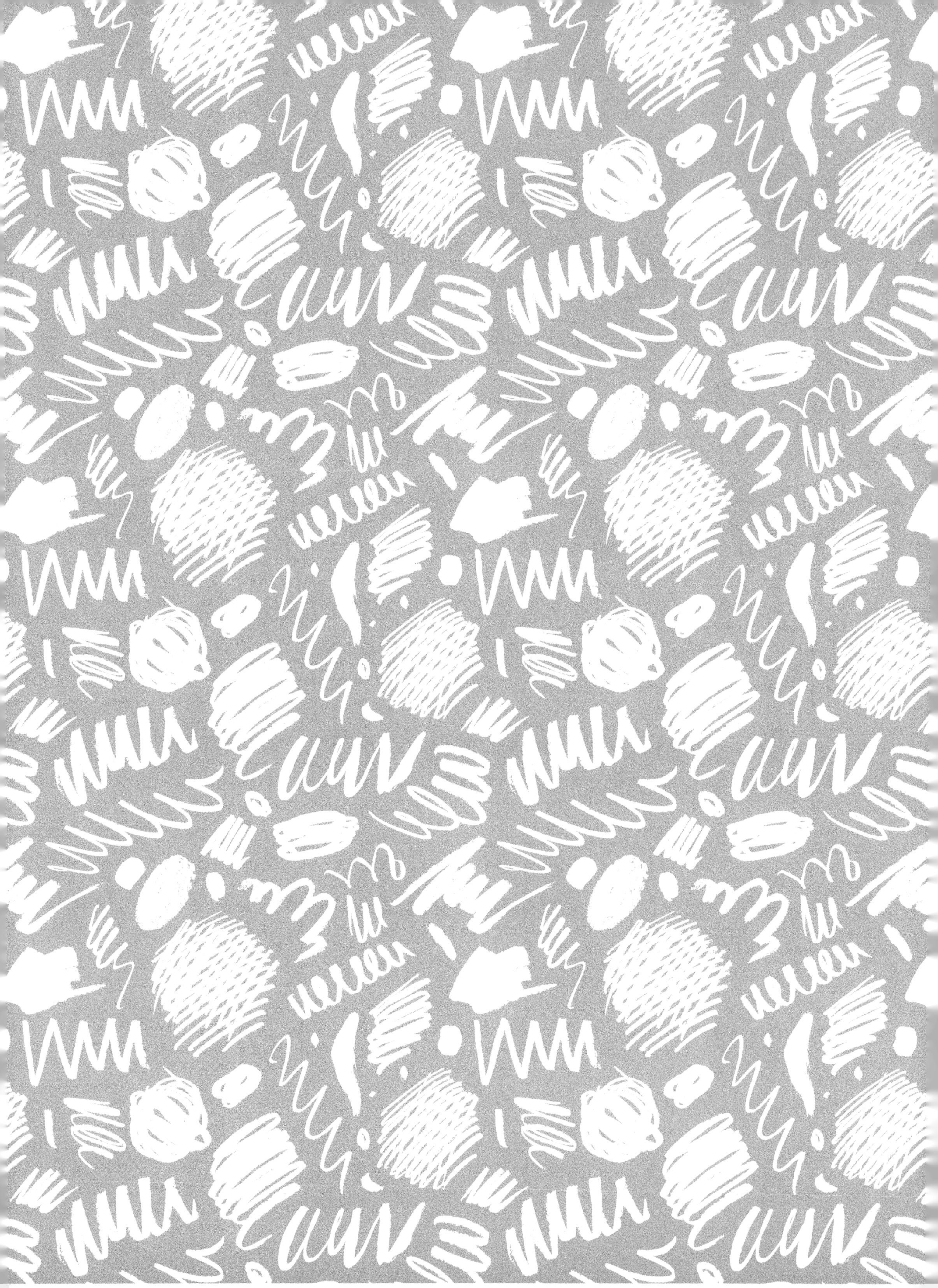

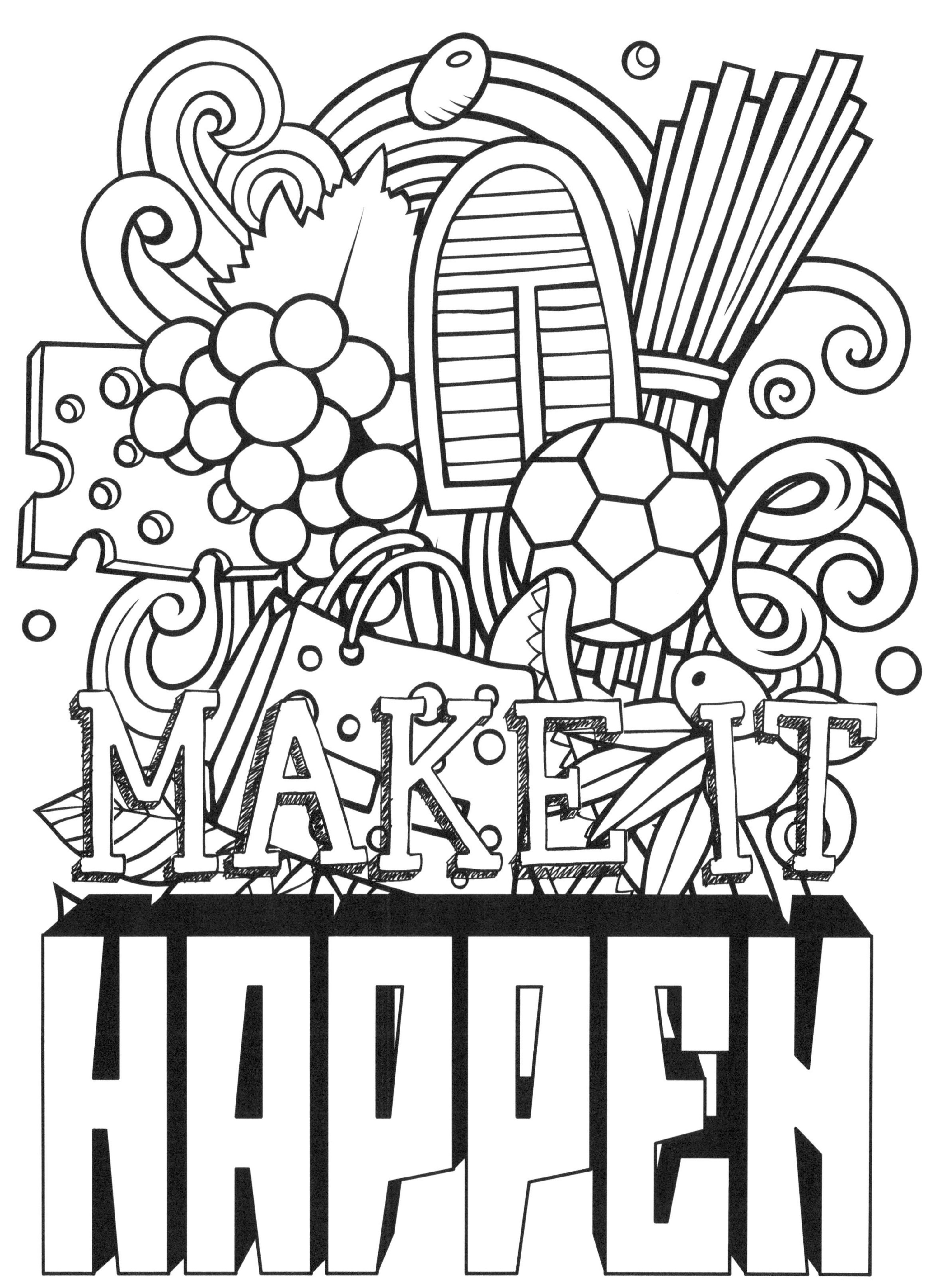

MAKE IT
HAPPEN

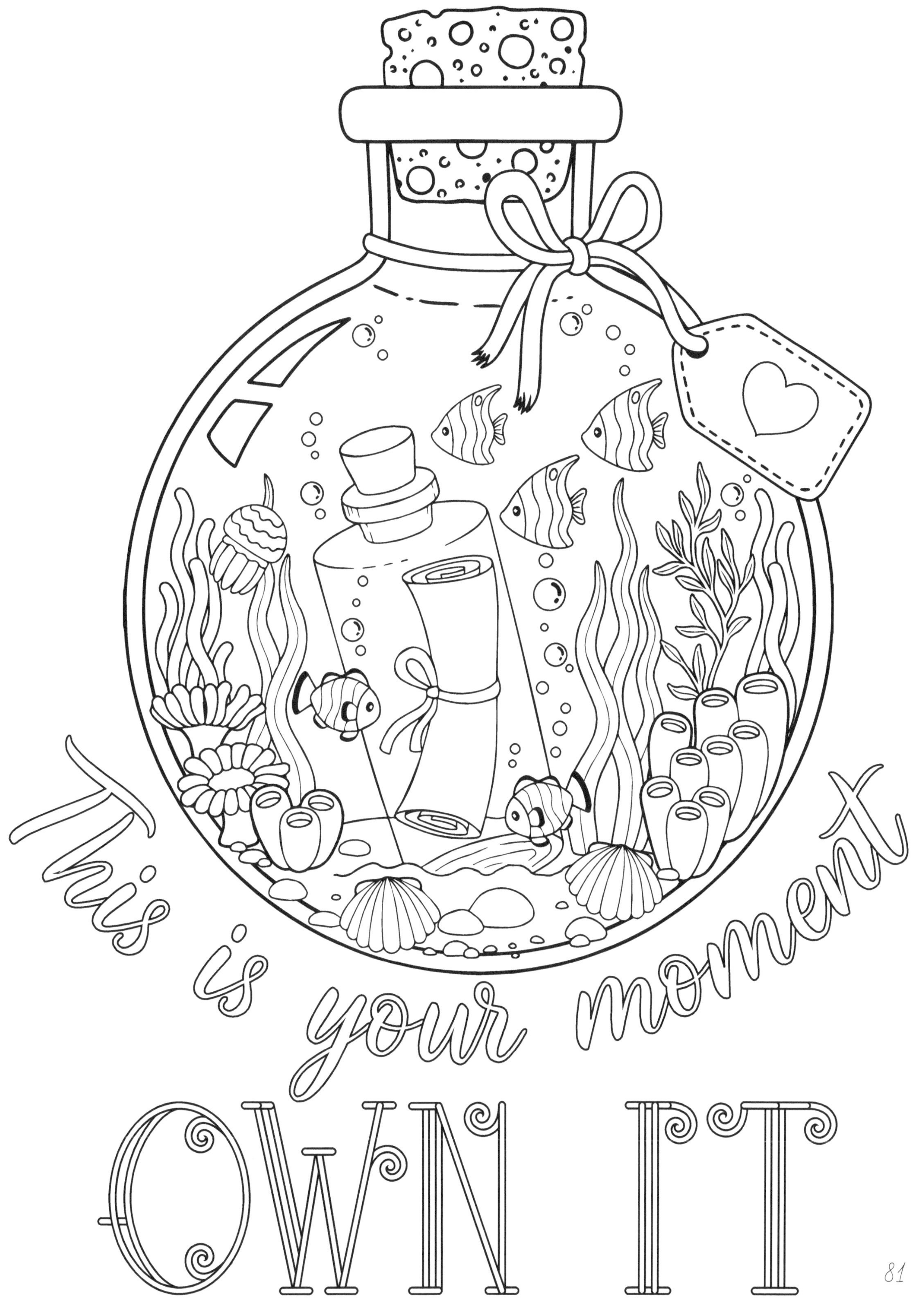

This is your moment
OWN IT

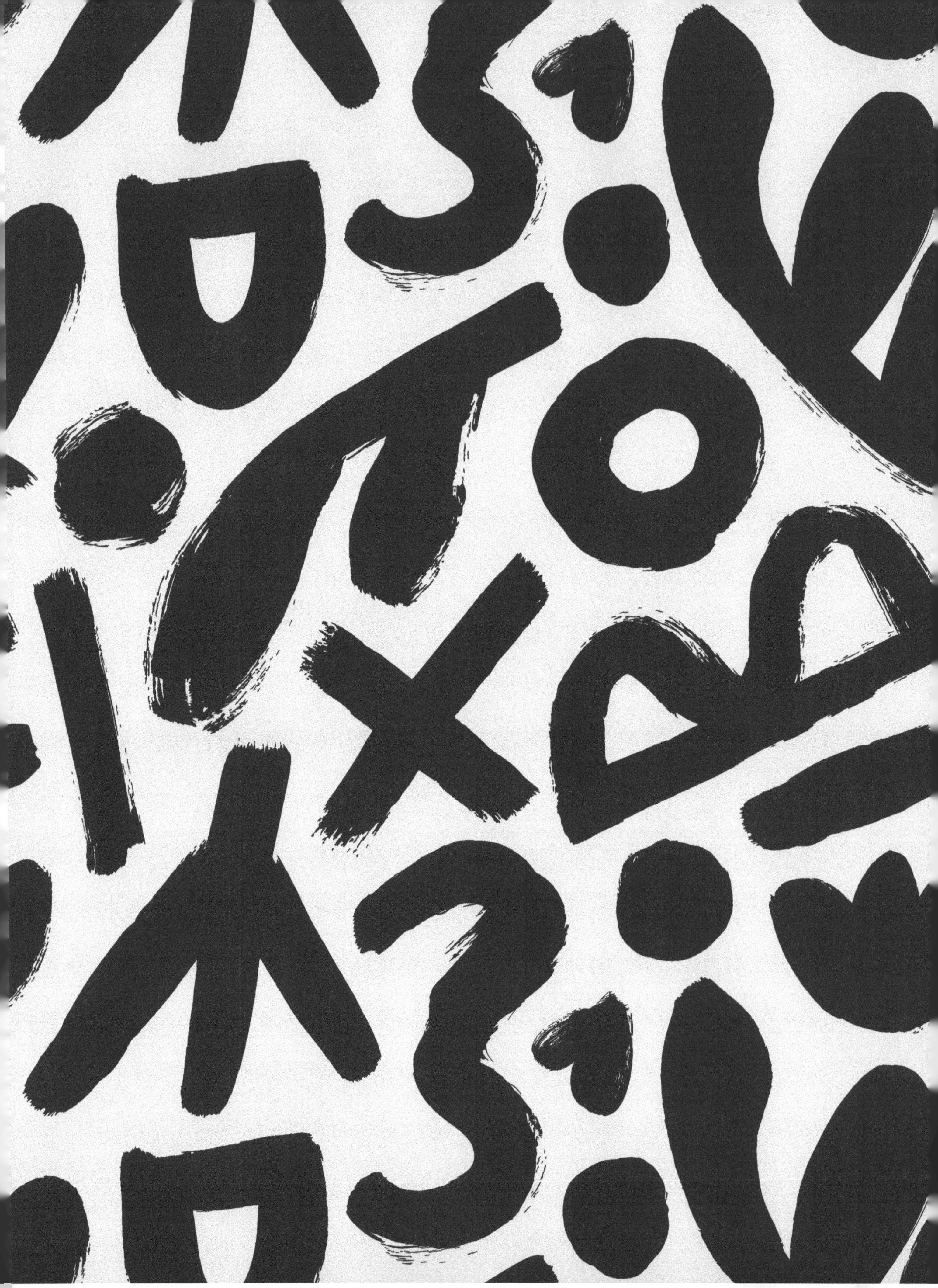

THERE
iS NO
LiMiT

WRITE
YOUR
OWN
STORY

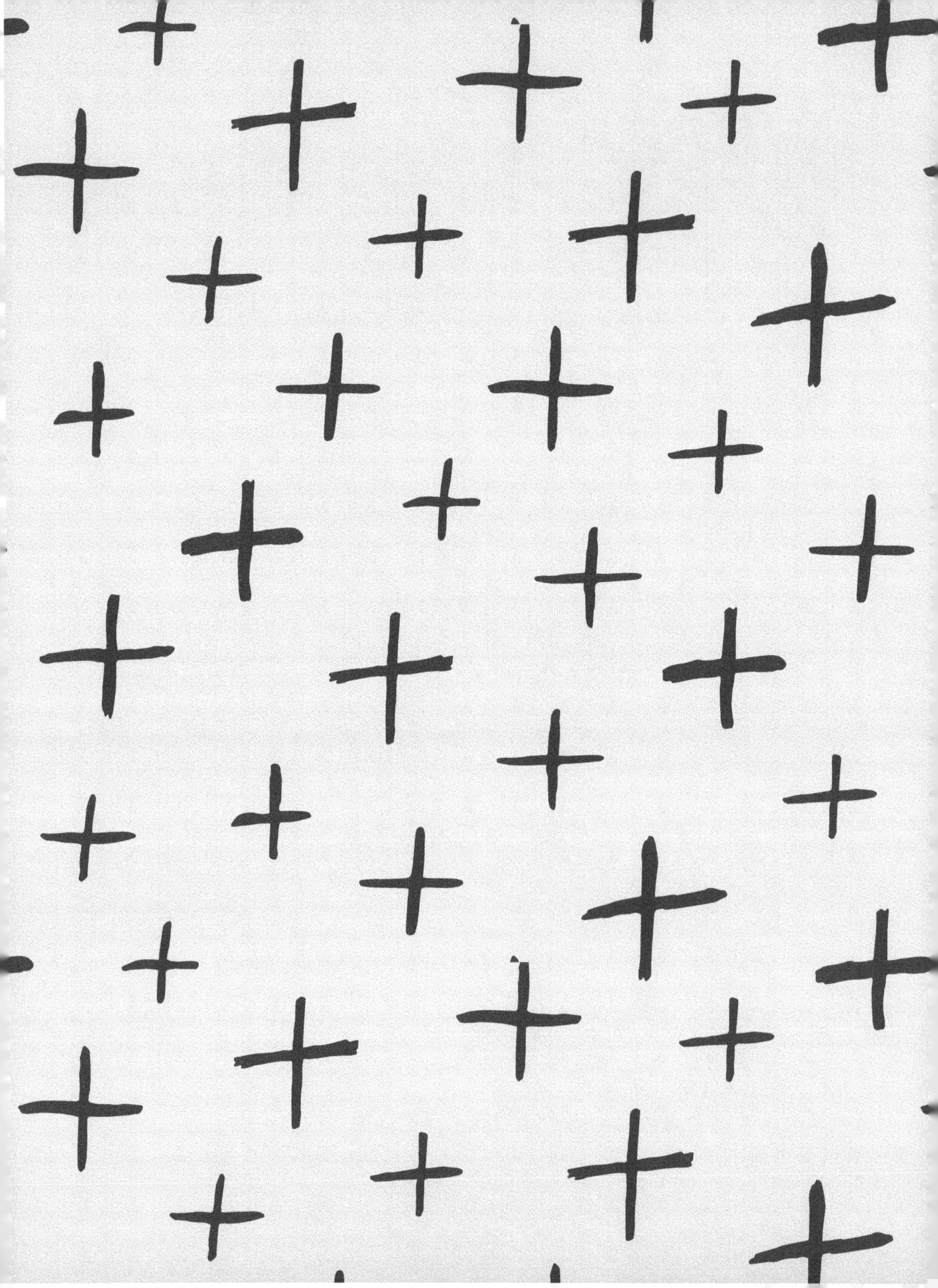

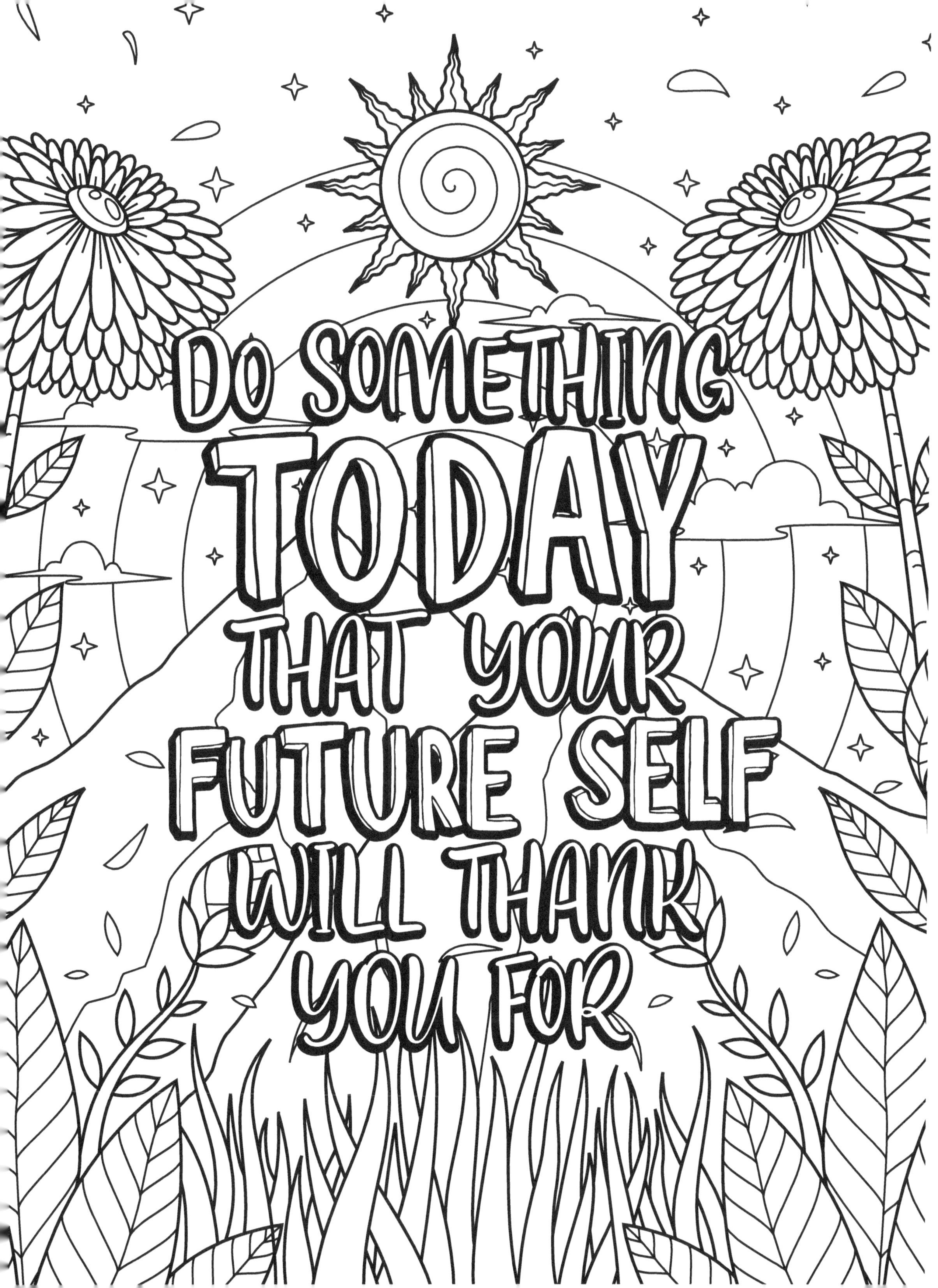

Do Something
TODAY
THAT YOUR
FUTURE SELF
WILL THANK
YOU FOR

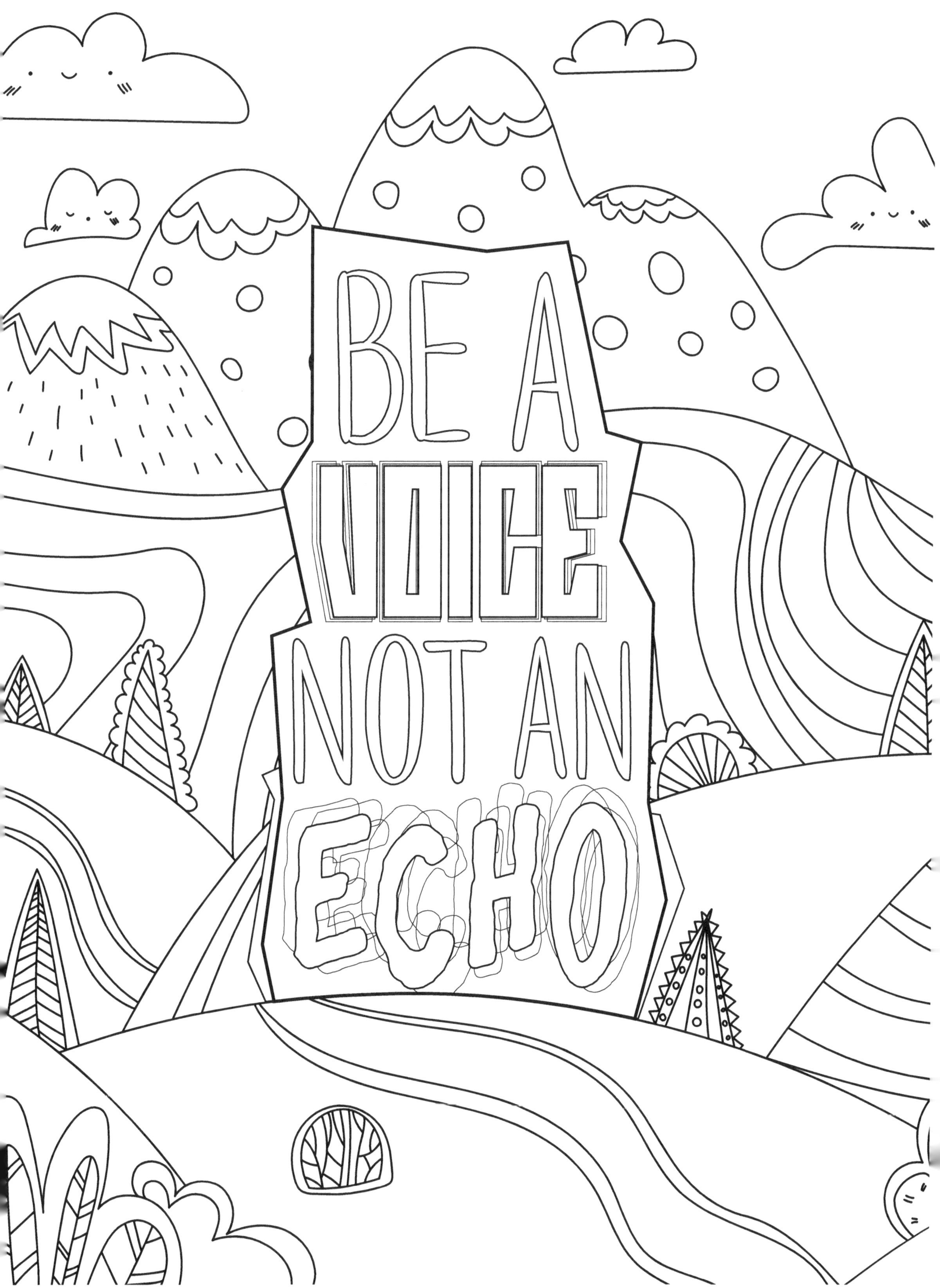

BE A
VOICE
NOT AN
ECHO

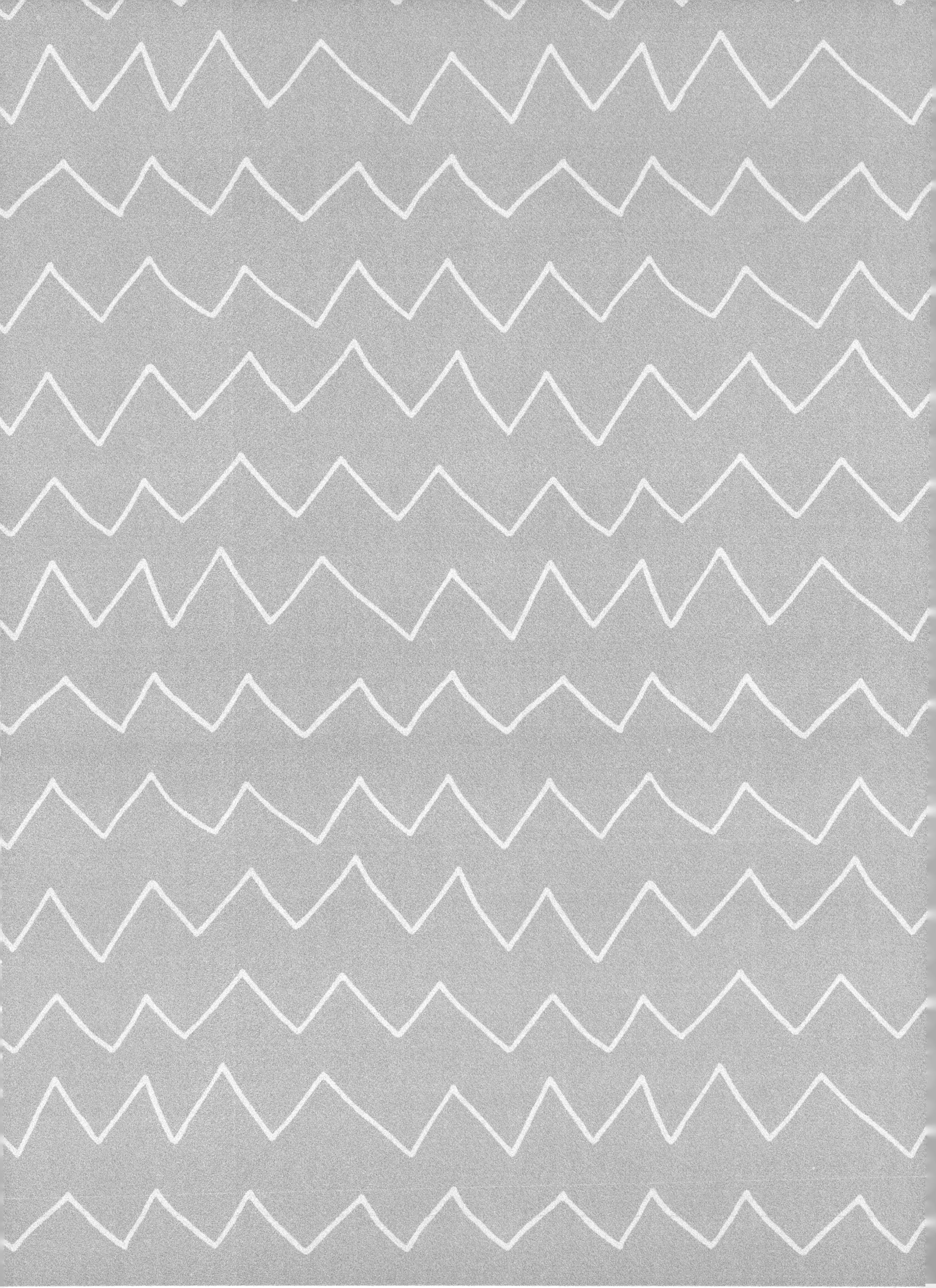

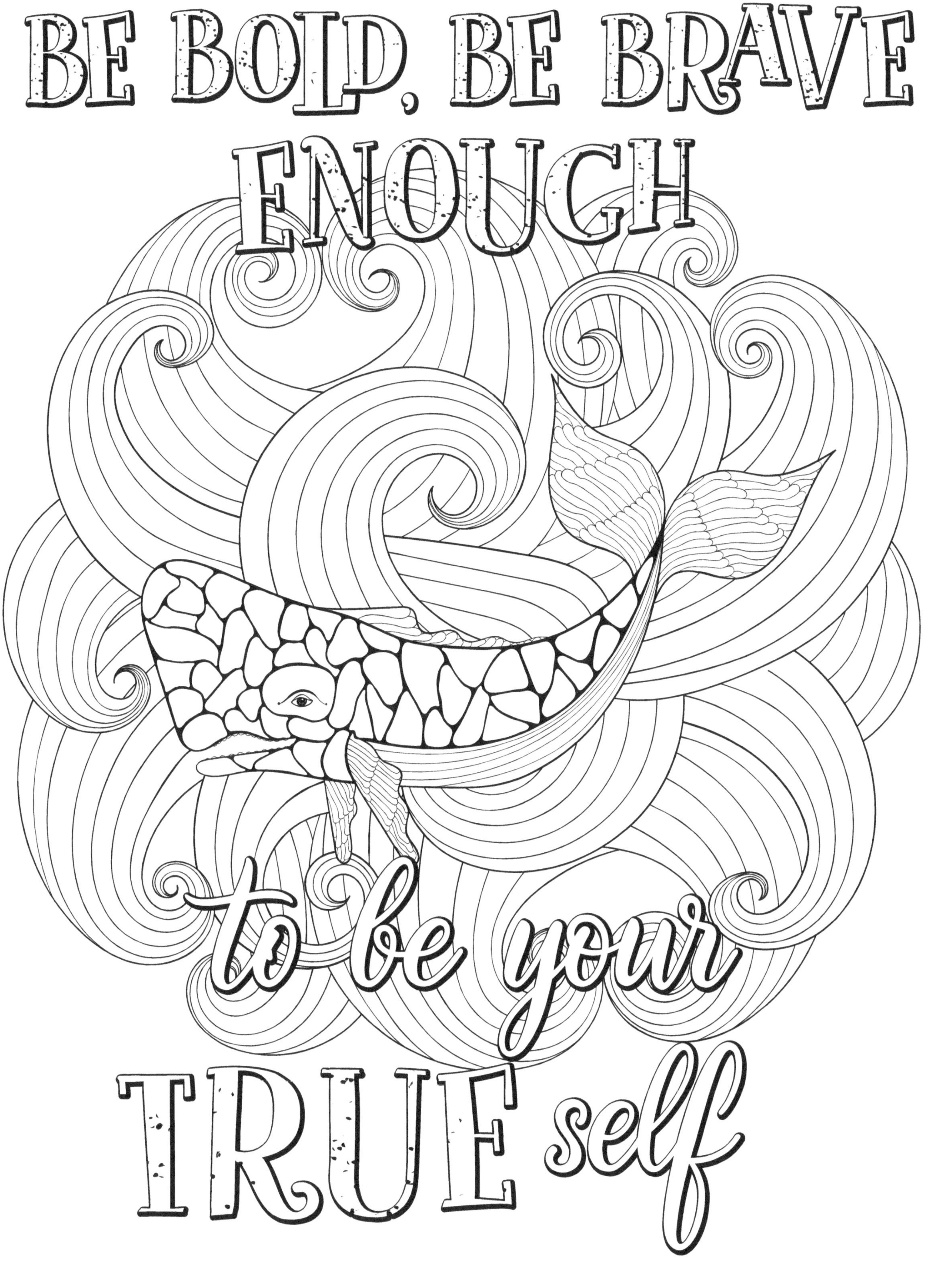

BE BOLD, BE BRAVE
ENOUGH
to be your
TRUE self

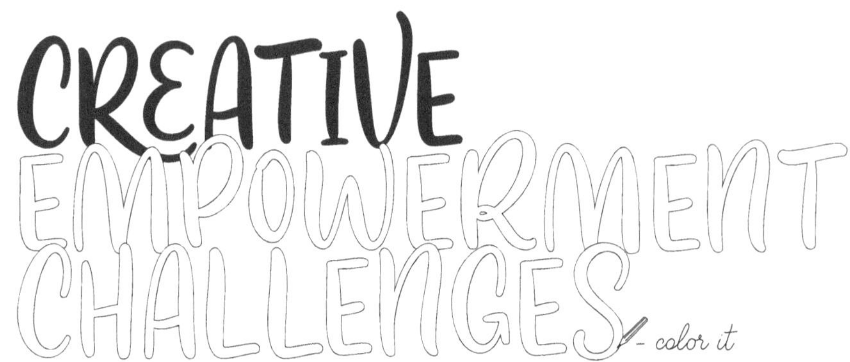


The words you speak to yourself have more impact than what the world tells you. In this chapter, practice empowering yourself by writing down your strengths in the style you have learned.

You can also try combining the styles or creating your own. This is the space where your creativity will be used for empowerment.

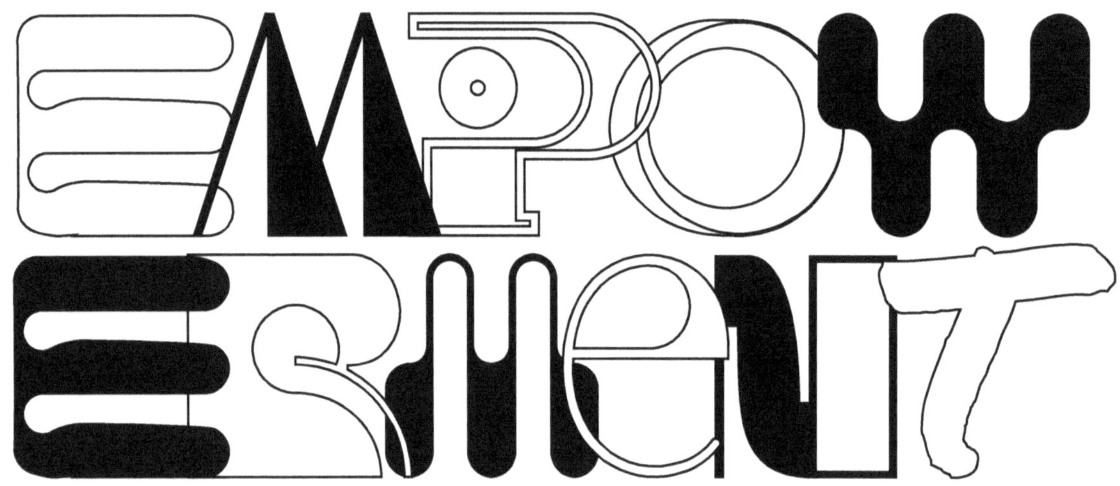

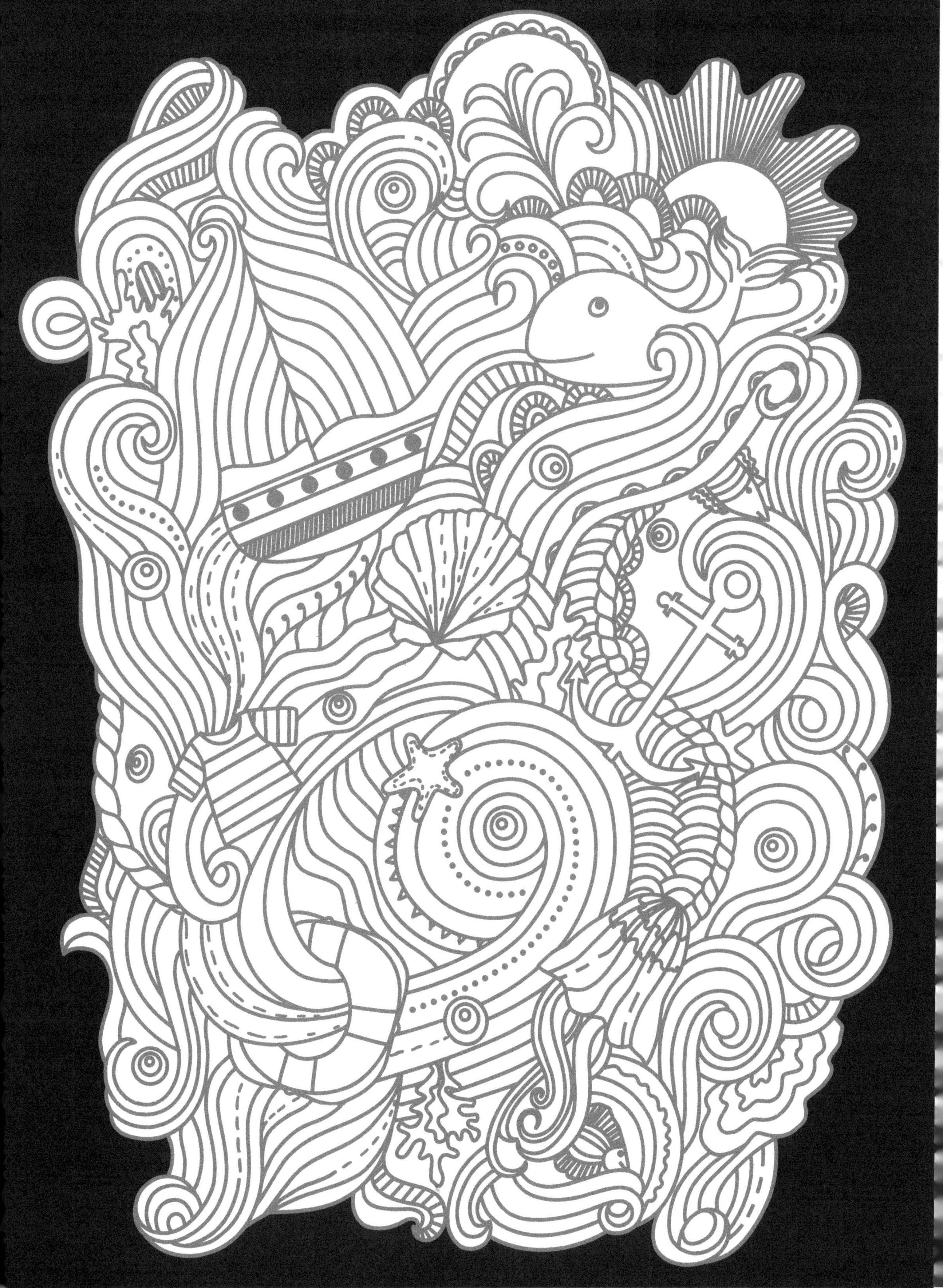

Now write down the strengths that you want to develop. Draw and color them in a way that will excite you as you take steps to self-empowerment.

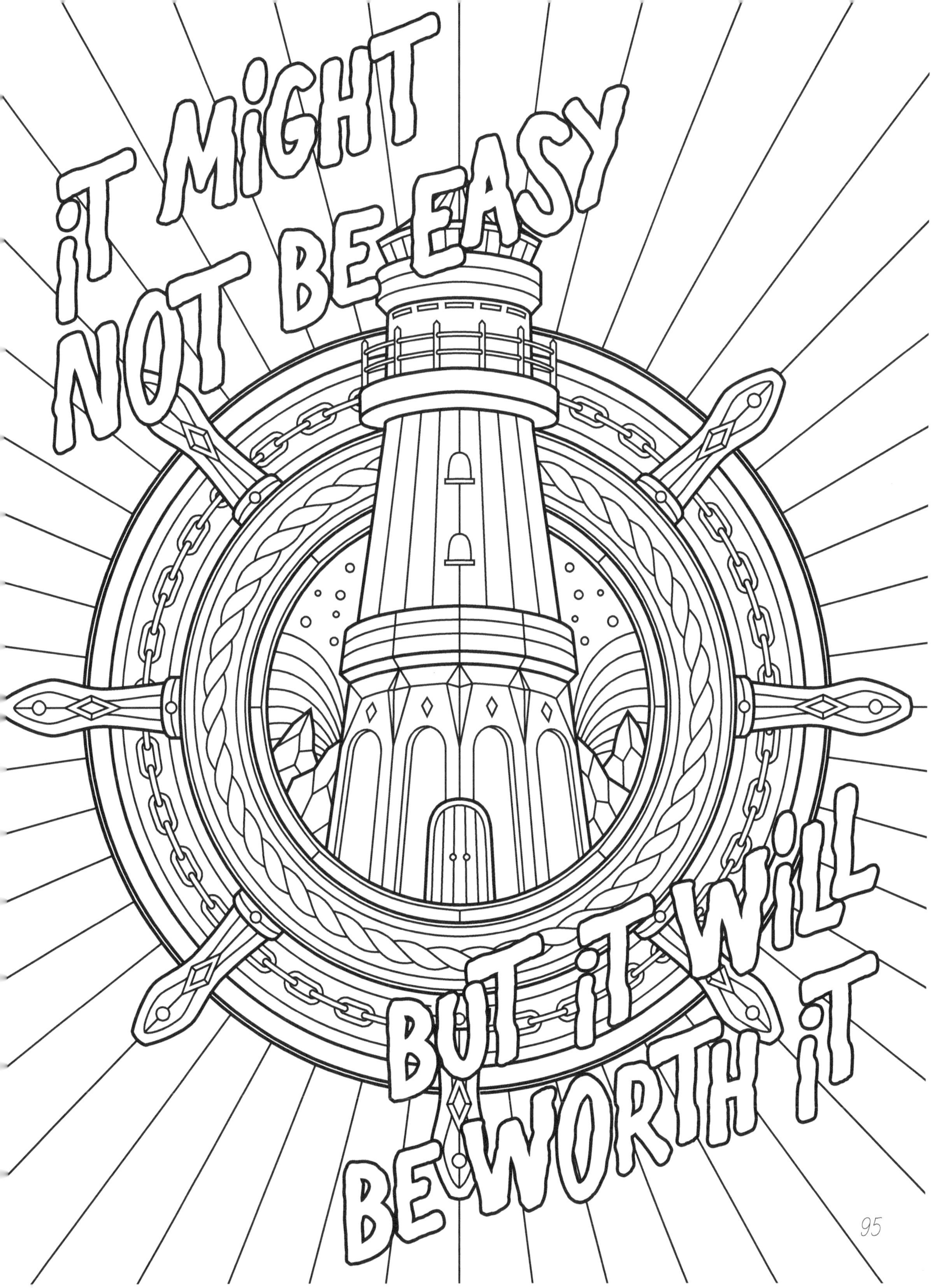

IT MIGHT NOT BE EASY
BUT IT WILL BE WORTH IT

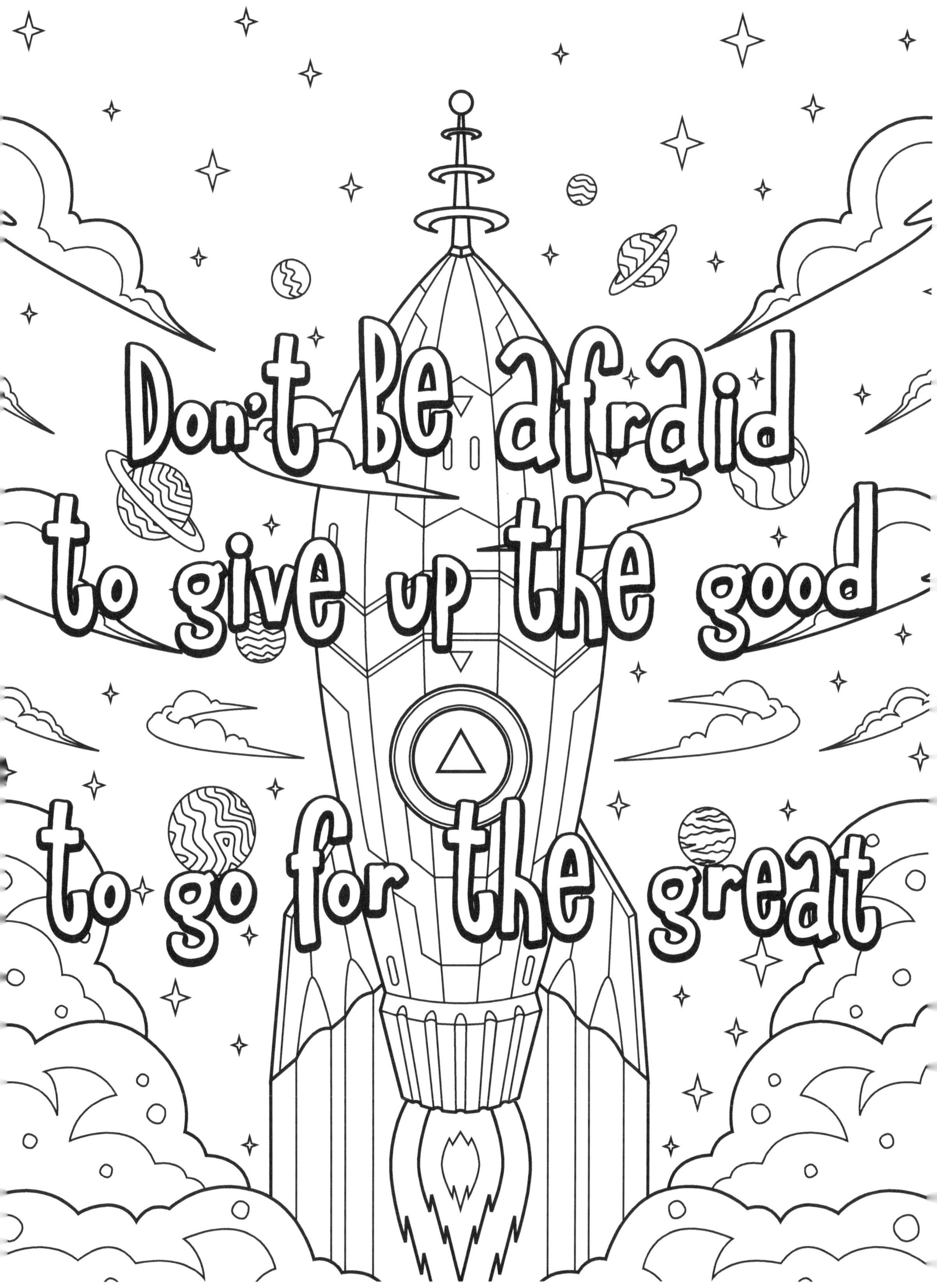

Don't be afraid
to give up the good
to go for the great

On the following pages, write a letter to someone you want to empower. It can be a family member or a friend — someone who needs the encouragement that you can give. Use your own style and creativity to convey your message.

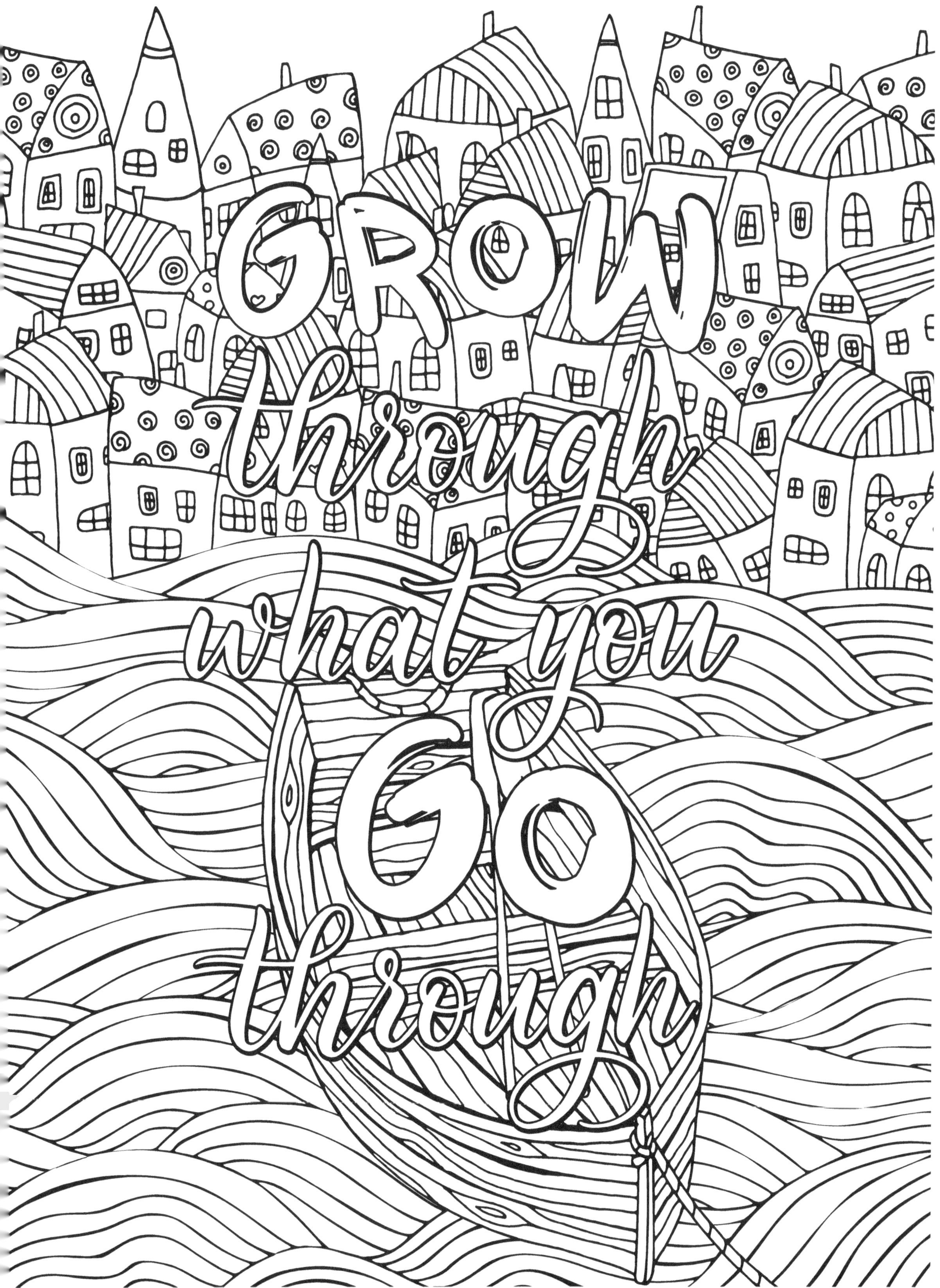

GROW
through
what you
GO
through

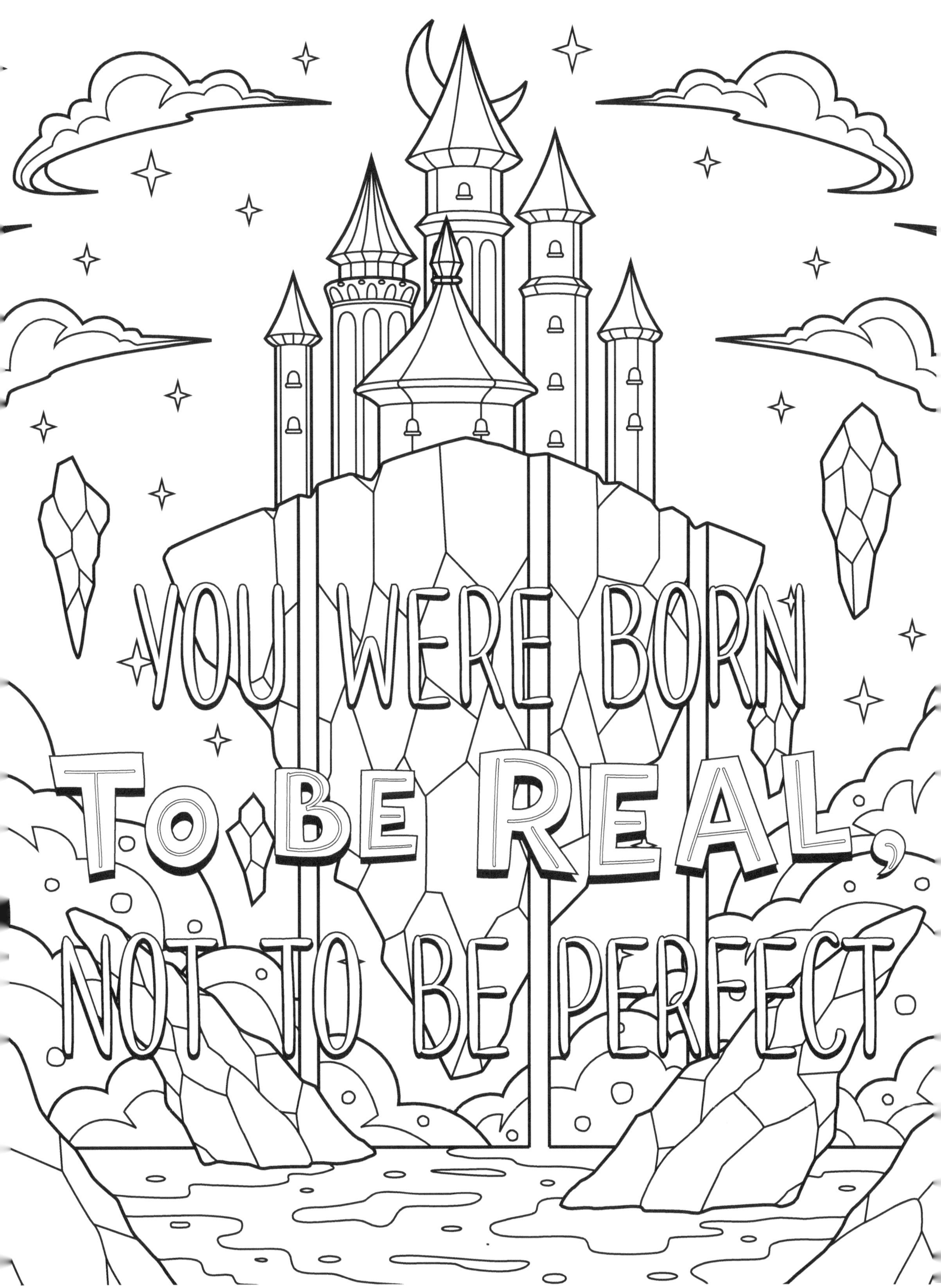

YOU WERE BORN
TO BE REAL,
NOT TO BE PERFECT

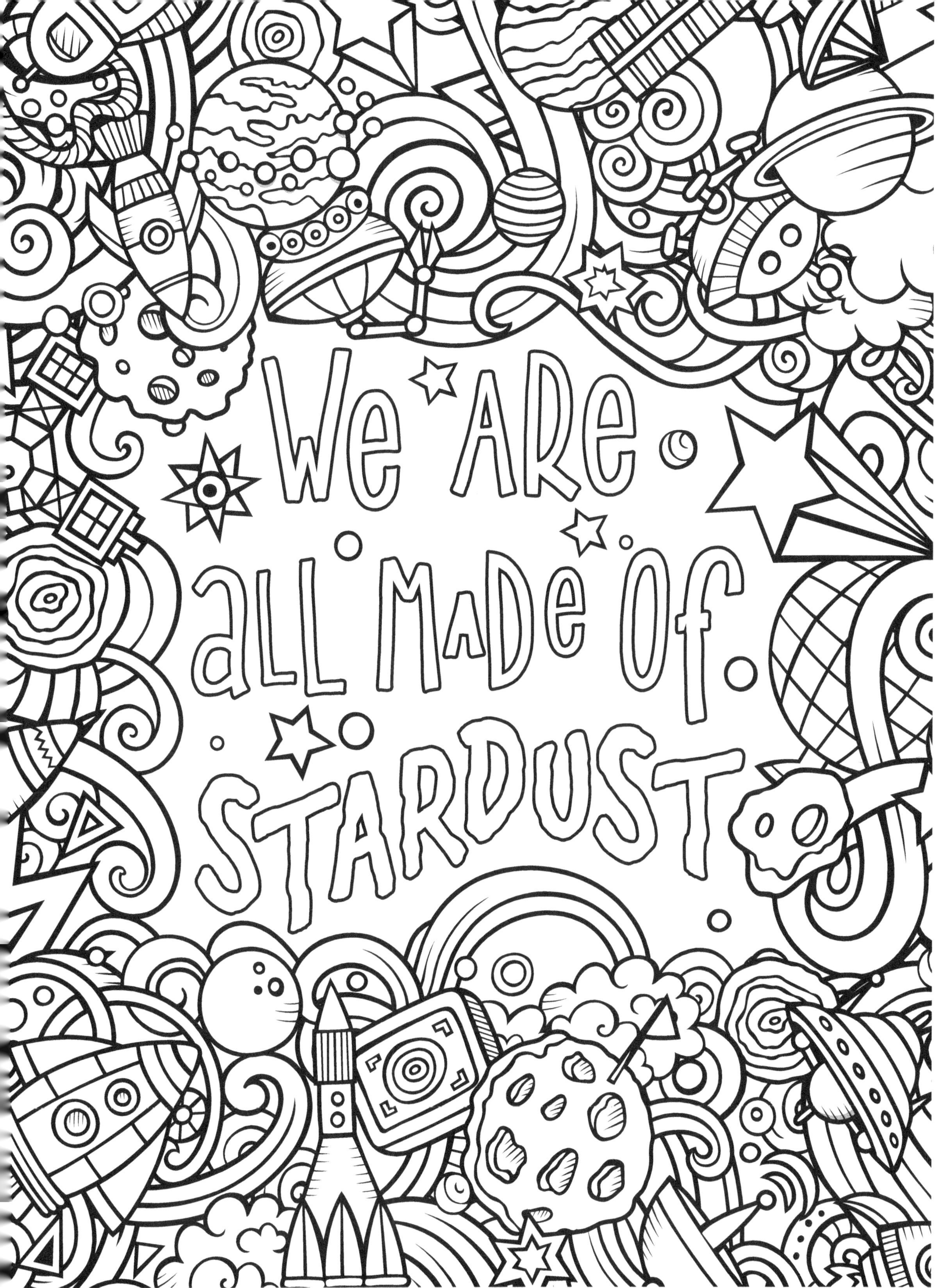

We are
all made of.
STARDUST

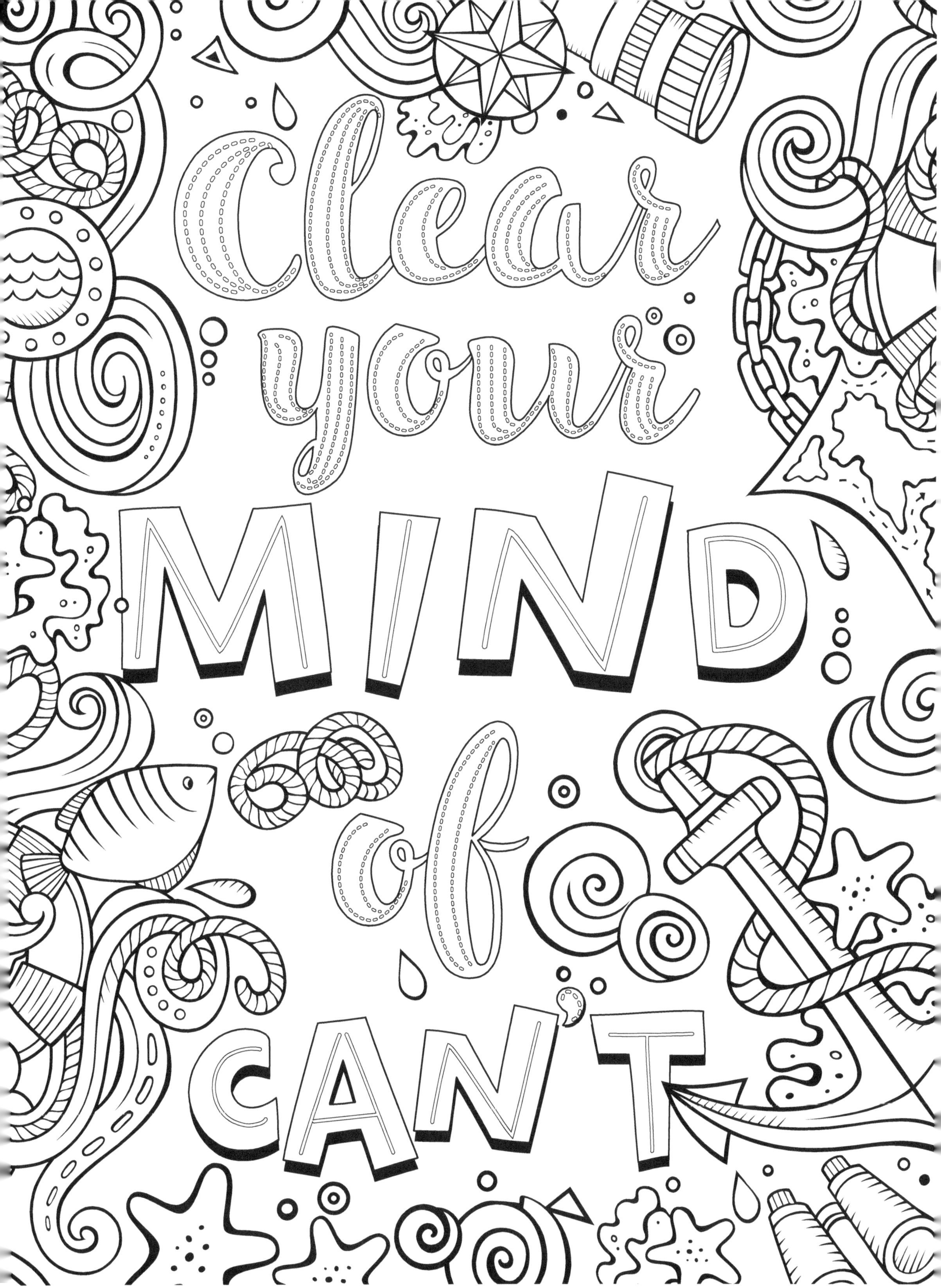

Clear
your
MIND
of
CAN'T

Now write another letter, this time to your future self. In the letter, write down how you will reach the freedom and power you want to embody in the coming months. Congratulate yourself on already reaching your goal. Remember that you will be reading this letter to yourself in the next few months.

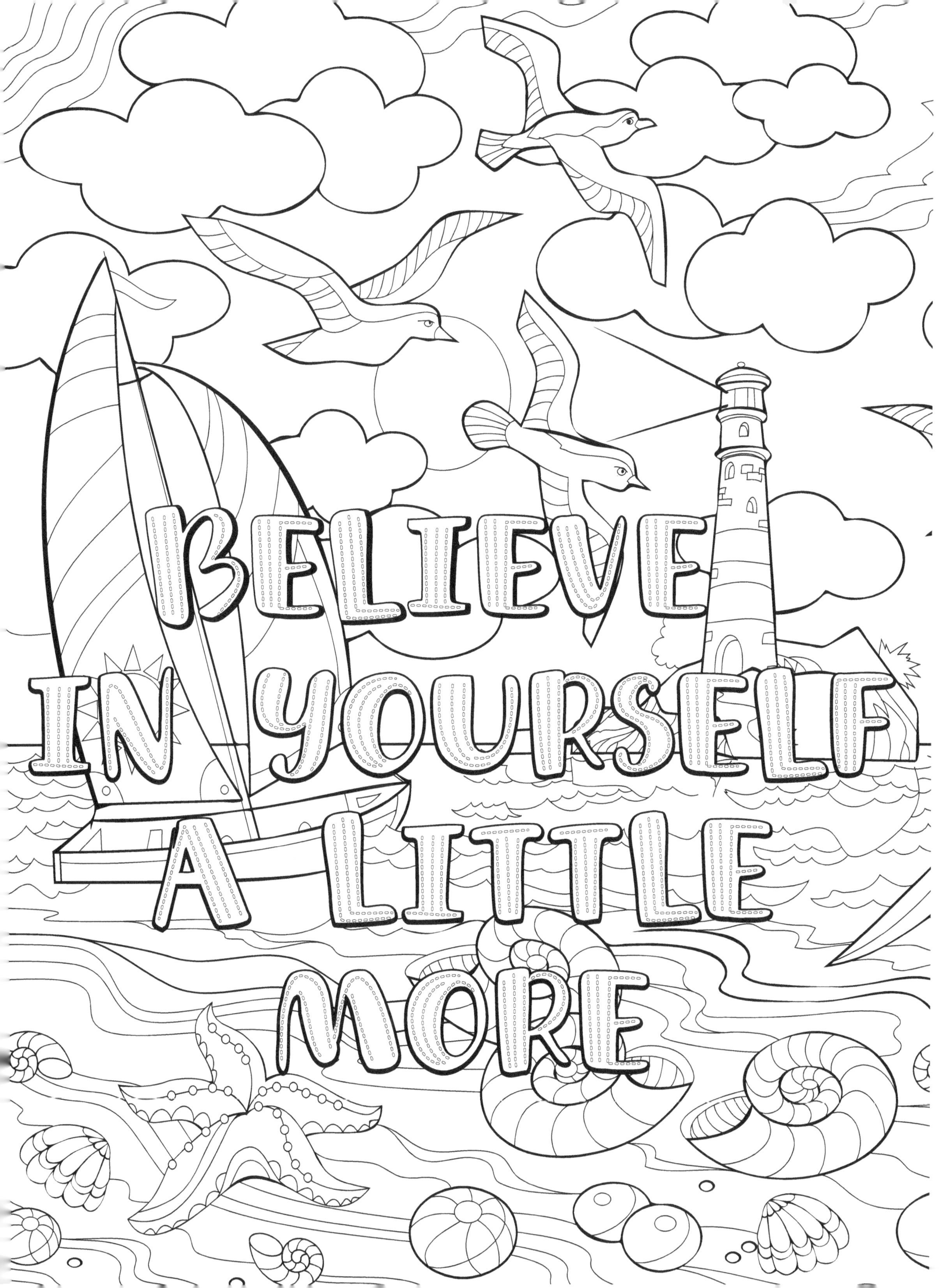

BELIEVE
IN YOURSELF
A LITTLE
MORE

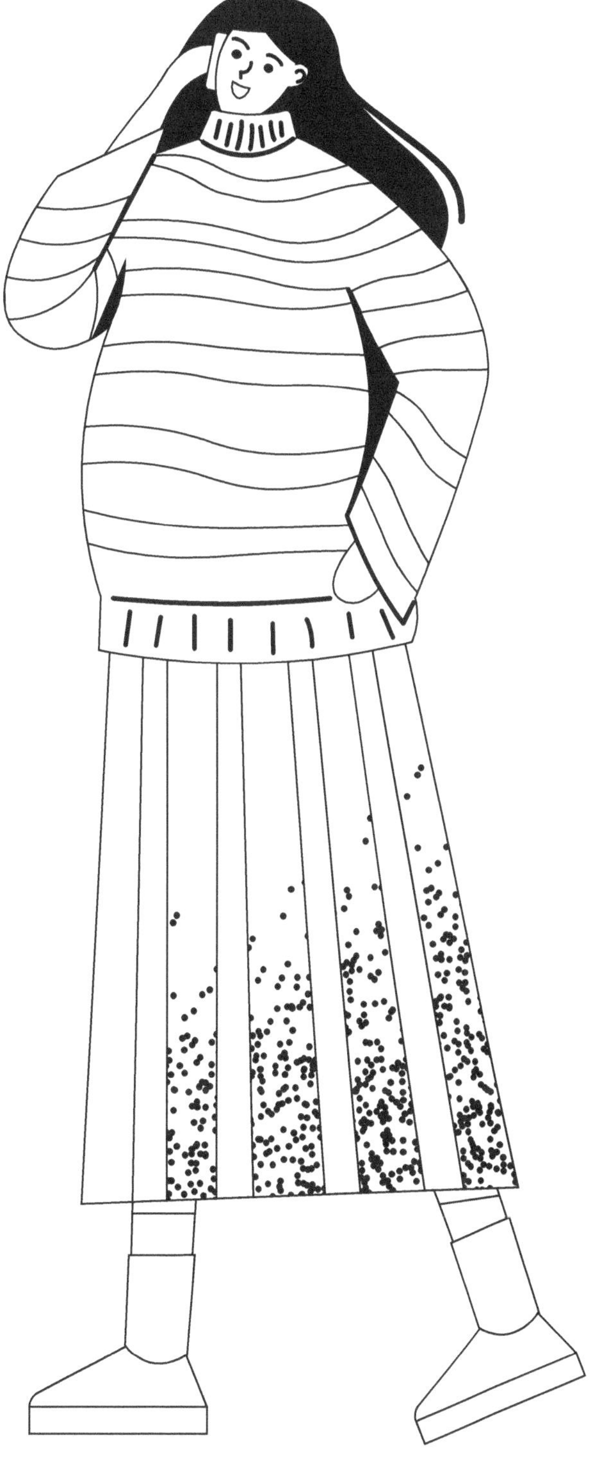

# REFLECTION AND GROWTH

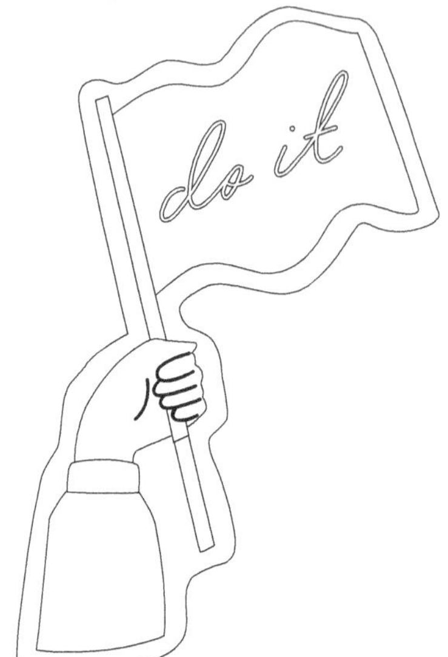


Congratulations! You've reached the end of your journey with *Letters of Empowerment*, and we hope you've experienced growth in both your lettering skills and self-confidence. As you've practiced various lettering styles, experimented with colors, and explored positive affirmations and your strengths, you've taken essential steps towards embracing the power of self-confidence and self-esteem in your life.

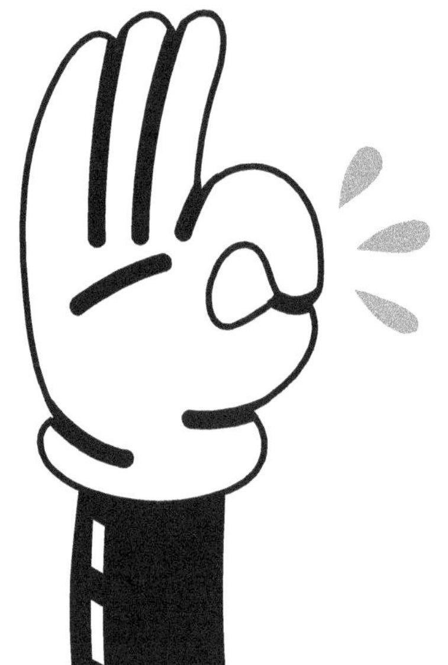

Now is the perfect time to pause and reflect on your achievements throughout this book. What have you learned about yourself? How have your lettering and coloring skills improved? How has your self-confidence grown? Use the space provided here to jot down your thoughts and celebrate your accomplishments. Remember, personal growth is an ongoing process, and it's essential to acknowledge your progress.

So, keep practicing and applying the lessons you've learned in *Letters of Empowerment* to your daily life. Remember that self-confidence and self-esteem are powerful tools that can propel you to greater heights. Thank you for sharing this journey with us, and we can't wait to see you flourish in this season of your life!

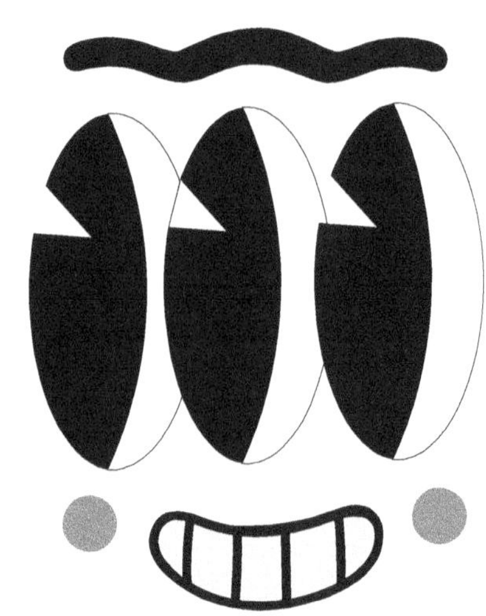



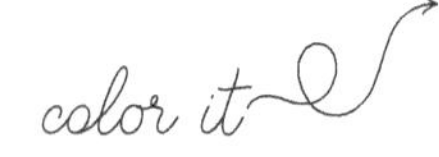

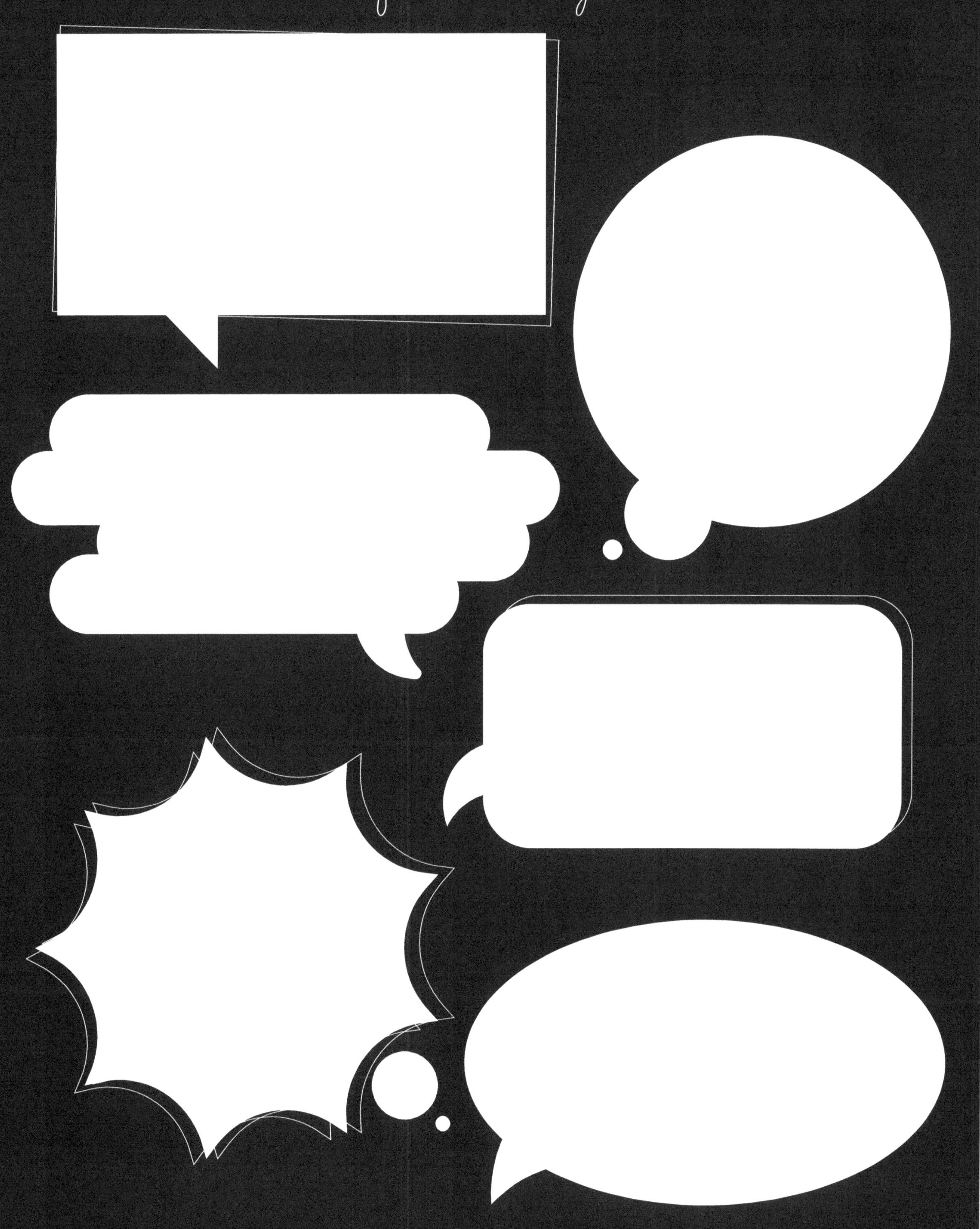

As a final exercise, write a letter to your new and more empowered self, encouraging you to keep doing the things you love and to never give up. Use the lettering styles you've learned and be creative!

The adventure continues! Express your emotions through different lettering styles and learn more about who you are and what makes you YOU!

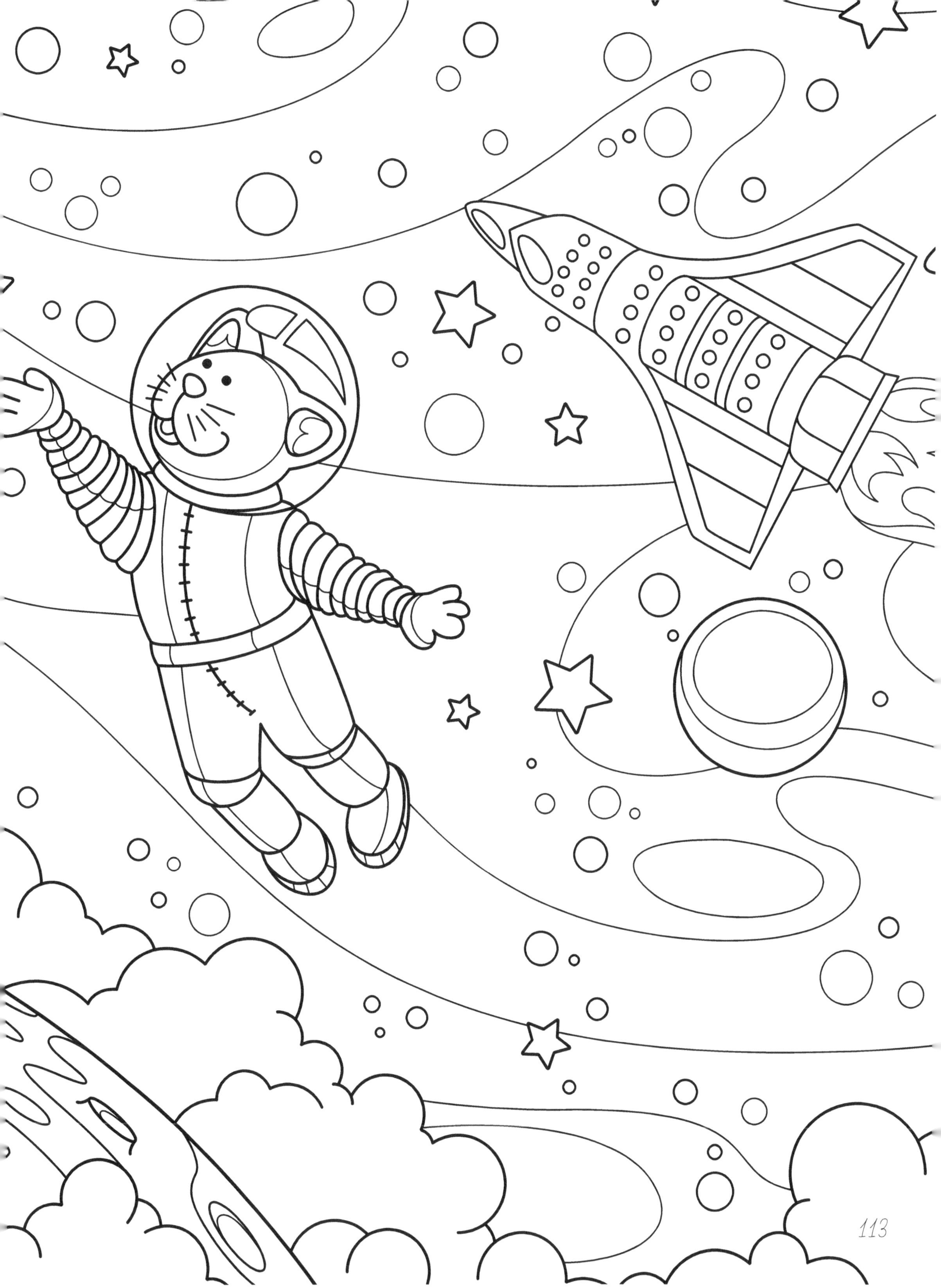

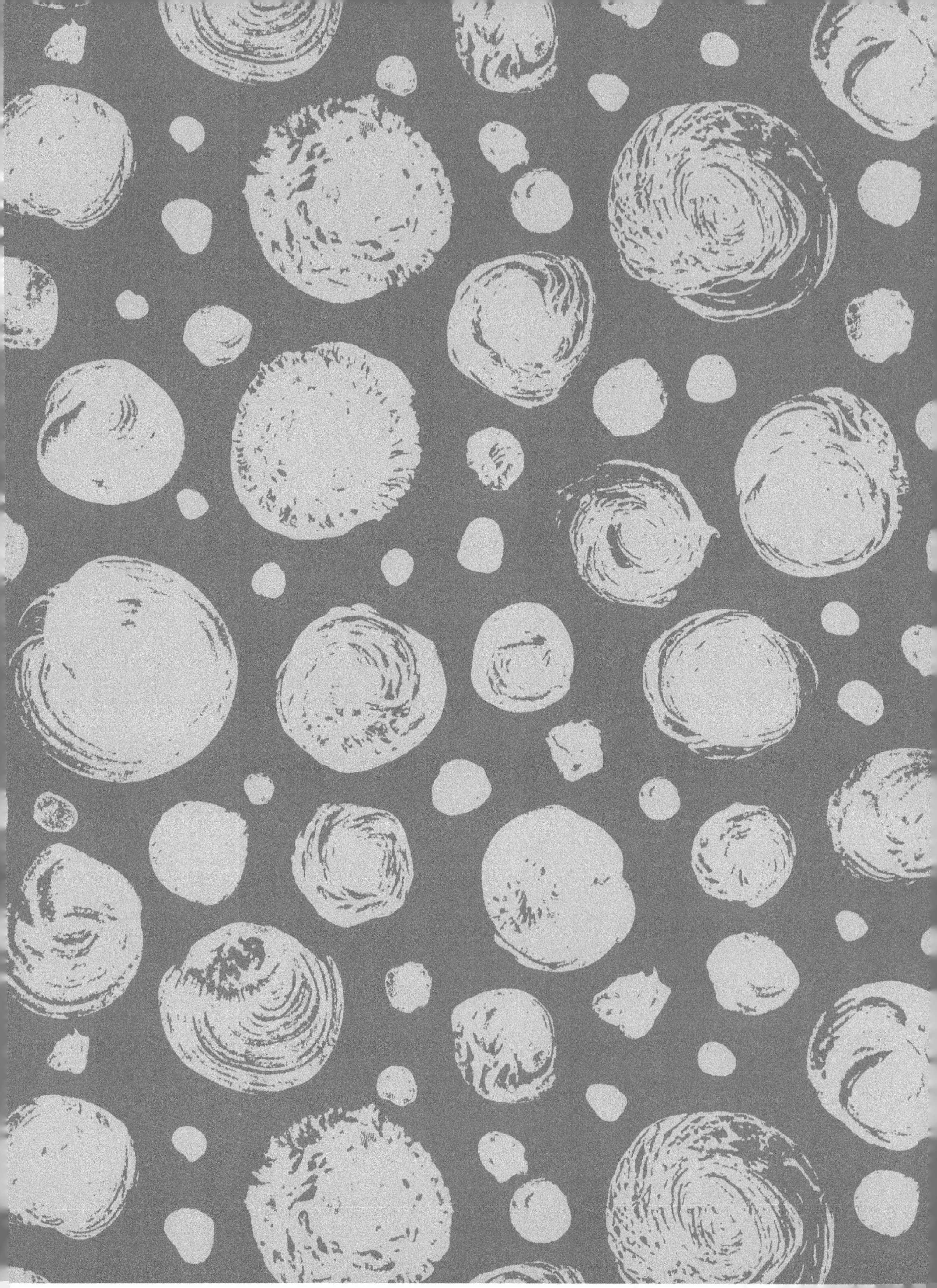